OH BEHAVE!

Reinforcing Successful Behaviors at Work With Consequences

**By Bruce Moeller & Craig Muller
With Andrew Goldsmith**

**ASPATORE
BOOKS**

Published by Aspatore Books, Inc.
For information on bulk orders, sponsorship opportunities or any other questions please email store@aspatore.com.

First Printing, 2002
10 9 8 7 6 5 4 3 2 1

ISBN 1-58762-112-6

Cover design by Kara Yates

Material in this book is for educational purposes only. This book is sold with the understanding that neither any of the authors or the publisher is engaged in rendering legal, accounting, investment, or any other professional service.

This book is printed on acid free paper.

A special thanks to all the individuals that made this book possible.

The views expressed by the individuals in this book do not necessarily reflect the views shared by the companies they are employed by (or the companies mentioned in this book).

About Aspatore Books
Business Intelligence From Industry Insiders
www.Aspatore.com

Aspatore Books publishes only the biggest names in the business world, including C-level (CEO, CTO, CFO, COO, CMO, Partner) leaders from over half the world's 500 largest companies and other leading executives. Aspatore Books publishes the Inside the Minds, Bigwig Briefs, ExecEnablers and Aspatore Business Review imprints in addition to other best selling business books and journals. By focusing on publishing only the biggest name executives, Aspatore Books provides readers with proven business intelligence from industry insiders, rather than relying on the knowledge of unknown authors and analysts. Aspatore Books focuses on publishing traditional print books, while our portfolio company, Big Brand Books focuses on developing areas within the book-publishing world. Aspatore Books is committed to providing our readers, authors, bookstores, distributors and customers with the highest quality books, book related services, and publishing execution available anywhere in the world.

OH BEHAVE!

Reinforcing Successful Behaviors at Work With Consequences

Table of Contents

Chapter 1
Introduction

Everything an organization does begins and ends with people.

Your employees are the most important capital you have. How you manage them should take priority over everything except customers – and even they are a manifestation of how you treat your employees. But most companies do not actually function that way. Why not? Because most companies can't quantify the benefits of their human capital. There are no numbers to look at. You can do satisfaction surveys, but there is a reliability gap – many of us have a hard time believing those numbers.

Even so, regardless of your rank in your company, from CEO to factory lineman, you have seen morale grow and deteriorate. Layoffs can crush employees' spirits in days; staff meetings can get out of hand in minutes. It can take weeks for things to get back together.

The value of human capital has only increased in recent years. A recent study quoted Baruch Lev, of New York University's Stern School of Business, as saying that the assets and liabilities listed on a company's balance sheet now account for only 60 percent of its real market value (*First Break All the Rules*, Marcus Buckingham and Curt Coffman, Simon & Schuster, 1999). The change has come because we have transitioned from a manufacturing economy to a service company. In a service economy, your assets are not machines but people – and their intellectual capital.

Today's employees know their value, especially in a tight labor market. According to Gartner Group's January 2001 report *Managing Human Capital in the New-Economy Enterprise*, employees now view the employment relationship as a way to manage personal goals – an idea that would have stunned the men in gray flannel suits and their bosses.

In this environment companies need to encourage each employee individually: assigning the right tasks, using the most effective types of instruction, and rewarding success in the different ways that will inspire different employees.

Behavioral science can show managers how to do all these things.

A program based in behavioral science will identify and reward your top performers and make sure they feel appreciated. They'll want to stay on the job and do the job better. Such a program will also identify what knowledge or skills employees lack, enabling you to make up that difference by giving them extra training in those specific areas. In the past companies would send everyone to a generalized training course. What would happen is that the company would spend a lot of money, and the employees would spend a lot of time on training that would not necessarily fit with what they needed. So the whole exercise became a waste of resources.

Behavioral science will ensure that the CEO's agenda proliferates throughout an organization. Most CEOs do not have the luxury of really knowing if their vision is truly being translated correctly throughout the company. Behavioral science, properly applied, allows that to happen. It takes that intangible idea that the CEO wants the company to be and turns it into a reality by identifying what its values are.

What is a customer centric value, for example, or saying you want to be the best? It's great to say that in a strategic sense, but what does that really mean? How do you translate that into a measurable activity? That's what behavioral science allows you to do, by translating the vision into distinct, measurable activities that every employee must carry out.

Incentives are a rudimentary form of behavioral science. Managers who haven't been trained in leadership or don't know anything about behavior look at using incentives as if they were part of a loyalty program. Let's give someone a charcoal grill for accomplishing this result, they'll say. The charcoal grill has some merit, but usually companies hand them out based on results and not on behavior. There is a place for rewarding results, but behavioral science tells us that it's behavior that is going to get you the long-term increase in the bottom line.

The key concept here is behavior change management. The benefits are improved performance and employee retention. With behavioral science you look at the results you want and then look at the behaviors that are needed to get the results. It's the behaviors that you're after. You'll stimulate activity, and you'll have a way to measure the results. With rewards for employees who act in ways that support the CEO's vision, your company can celebrate itself down to the individual.

You can measure performance up the ladder as well. Buckingham and Coffman's study, based on interviews with more than a million employees, found that an employee's immediate manager is the one with the most influence over job satisfaction and, hence, job performance. Often, senior management is out of touch with what is going on with the rest of the organization. If executives knew that certain managers were causing good employees to leave – or if they even knew they had good employees – then they would do something about it. Right now, in most cases, they don't know that. Who is watching the henhouse? Behavioral science can. It's not only good for monitoring employees' skills and development, but it's good for managers. You can create a reporting system that closes the loop and will show you which managers provide feedback and are using the system by rewarding and recognizing the employees. You can see who isn't and go talk to them. You can have the manger evaluated by peers, the boss, and employees to give you a better, holistic view of how this person is running the department.

If you work in a public company, behavioral science can improve more than just your profits. The Gartner Group report notes that when stock analysts look at a company, they look at financial numbers, but often the biggest differentiator is good will and the invisible strengths that a company has. Is that company the best place to work? Are employees happy? Do they stay there? Does senior management care about them? How gregarious are the CEO and president? All of those things play a big role in how analysts measure a company and all of those things have to do with becoming more people oriented, not just a focus on hard assets.

Technology is a key tool in many areas of business today, and behavioral science programs are no different. One of the most important factors in employing behavioral science's principles is providing reinforcement or recognition as soon as possible when somebody performs the relevant behaviors. In the past there were old methods of waiting until the end of the month to reward people, or it was so impromptu that it didn't seem that there was any true organization to it at all.

Electronic monitoring can dramatically shorten the time frame in which people are recognized for doing good things. You have to catch them in the act of doing something right and reward it right there.

Behavioral science is literally an operating system for human behavior. Any corporate goal that you can think of and takes human beings to execute can be improved with this system – literally anything with a human. If I want to be more customer intimate, what does that mean to the guy loading the truck, or the person in accounting when the phone rings? Answering these types of questions, filtering any imperative through the types of behaviors that would support it, is the key.

In today's world you have to take care of your people because they are really the asset that differentiates you from your competitors.

Chapter 2

Errors of the Past

Management has four key elements: planning, leading, organizing, and controlling. Managers have had endless systems for doing everything except for leading. There has never been a tool for leading.

Leading is about deciding what direction you are going to go in, and then getting your people to go in that direction. The most effective way to spur employees to go in the direction you've chosen – to modify their behavior – is to create consequences for their actions. People do it on an informal, ad hoc basis all the time. But if you do it consciously and with a purpose, people will follow you.

Fads

Scientific measurements, total quality management, and most other management techniques are fads. None of these work unless employees want to do what needs to be done. You can't expect quality circles to work unless the people in the quality circles are actually doing something that adds value. They aren't going to do it unless there is a consequence for behaviors that add value.

You can be the best person in the shipping room and ship more boxes every day than anybody else. But if nobody comes up to you and tells you that you are doing a good job and recognizes you to reinforce that behavior, without a doubt, as a human, your behavior will decrease. To use a behavioral science term, it will become extinct. Your level of production will go down to the same level of production as anyone else's. Without the recognition, improvement – and even simple maintenance – doesn't happen.

You can have all the quality circles you want, and you can reengineer the department. You might get some benefits out of it. But they are all going to be short term if you don't work on an individual's behavior through recognition or through some immediate and certain consequence. If you don't get it in line and make it sustainable, then it isn't going to work on a long-term basis. Look at all these other methods. They have come and gone, and have all had short-term effects on companies – but they aren't sustainable.

All of these initiatives were very well conceived and executed, but almost all of them have withered. They are the ideas of the month, the latest theory of the CEO. If you don't align consequences so that they can be uniformly deployed and consistently reinforced, then you don't have people walking the talk. Typically companies give consequences annually, like a raise or a bonus. That's not what shapes behavior; immediate consequences do. That's why these things fail. They all sound good in the beginning, but all are missing immediate consequences. Let's consider one in detail: the balanced scorecard

The Balanced Scorecard

You measure the quality of your employees' compliance with procedures and operations. You measure customer satisfaction. You measure financial results, individual and team performance. But looking at each of these measurements individually will give you a very limited view of how your company, department or employee is performing.

The truth is that all of these factors work together to create a holistic view of an individual, or of the entire company – and that's the idea on which the balanced scorecard is based. The balanced scorecard is becoming a popular method for providing an accurate view of performance and its relationship to corporate strategy.

Balanced scorecards provide a comprehensive view of a company's overall performance, by integrating financial, operational, customer, and growth measures with other key performance indicators. Data is taken from quality monitoring systems, financial reports, and other evaluations such as manager observations. Each data component is weighted and integrated with the others to provide a holistic view of performance.

But wait! Something is missing! That's right, most balanced scorecards are missing a critical link: turning knowledge into action.

The Critical Missing Link

Leveraging the highest performance potential from a balanced scorecard requires an important link to be in place: the link between scorecard results and having a tool for acting on that information. Without this link, your balanced scorecard is just a more complete reporting device.

Most scorecards measure and integrate many different performance indicators, but few provide the ability to automate changes in activities or behavior that will affect performance or reinforce successful efforts. Typically, managers receive reports every day, yet department performance stays the same. This gap between scorecard results and execution leaves a wealth of untapped performance potential.

A systematic ability to apply immediate rewards and reinforcement empowers the scorecard not only to provide information, but to use that information to direct and focus employee efforts in real time. With automated rewards and recognition, employees execute in accordance with the information and the strategic goal. It's the link that executes immediate change so that things do change – for the better.

The facts are there: research conducted by the Hay Group and The McGraw-Hill Companies shows a strong correlation between linking reward systems with a balanced scorecard approach and improvements in performance management. Behavioral science has proven that people will repeat a desired behavior if that behavior is reinforced and rewarded.

By linking rewards to scorecard measurements, you will optimize the human effort of your employees and align them with your operations and desired results. In order to create better reporting systems, thoroughly review how managers and supervisors should engage that information to create positive change. Performance systems exist that can automate that execution and make balanced scorecards a total solution for improved performance.

If you could get someone to love working the way any of these fads such as TQM propose, then it would probably work. But then it is behavior management, and not TQM. That's the secret. A lot of companies today are getting into the secret, getting into individual behavior, rather than branding some sort of management technique and trying to put it into place. If you get somebody to love his or her job, then you've found the key to unlocking their potential.

The Old School

Managers can fail by relying on fads, or they can fail by relying on an old-fashioned military mentality. If your boss comes in and says that he doesn't care how you get something done, as long as you get it done, and if you don't you are out of the company, then when you go to your subordinate, you may use the same tone and strategy.

Some bosses tell middle managers they are being too nice because they're putting rewards on a bulletin board in the lunchroom. Some people think that the only way to get things done is to tell people to just do it.

When someone asks why, the answer is, "Because I said so." Maybe that's the way we handle our kids, and the way we were brought up. There is no time for an explanation – "I am the boss, and go do it because I pay you." We learn that same technique. The general manager says to the chief operating officer what he or she wants done. The chief operating officer goes out to the floor manager and says he wants that done, and it goes on down the line. It's now policy.

Praise has a bad rap in business. There is an unspoken consensus in the working world that of course people should work hard, that's what they get paid for, why should they be told they're doing a good job? In addition to this general anti-praise bias, senior executives are always "too busy," managers are afraid to praise people too frequently lest they be perceived as "soft," and supervisors are fearful of becoming known as pushovers.

The power of praise is that it reinforces, recognizes, and motivates desirable behavior. When you praise people, you make people feel good about what they did, good about themselves and good about their jobs. Effective praise is more than passing around a few indiscriminate warm fuzzies. It's about listening and looking for opportunities to recognize people. By focusing on what is going on around you, you will become more aware of the qualities that make your organization work: teamwork, cooperation, communication, and people. Almost magically, attitude improves and morale is bolstered. The best is yet to come: ultimately these recognized, energized people will prove to be the most productive in the organization.

Aside from improved attitudes, morale, and productivity – important benefits in themselves – there is another long-term, bottom-line benefit to recognizing and praising employees. *Sales and Marketing Management* magazine recently polled Fortune 1000 companies and found that the number one reason people leave their jobs is lack of appreciation and praise! Systematic, frequent praise becomes one of the most cost-effective tools to attract and retain valued workers.

There are four key qualities to effective people-pleasin' praise. It must be:

> *Sincere:* People sense sincerity and commitment. Sarcasm or a flip attitude will undermine your message and do more harm than good.
>
> *Immediate:* For the greatest effect, praise should occur as soon after the event as possible. Praising someone a month after the performance isn't nearly as effective as just after the fact.
>
> *Specific:* Saying "Good job on the report," won't work as well as, "I really appreciate your attention to detail on the report you did

for me last week. The facts were clear and it was error free. Thanks for your effort."

Meaningful: Meaningful praise ties the praise back to an individual's personality or qualities: "I really appreciate your attention to detail on the report you did for me last week. The facts were clear and it was error free. It's great having such a thorough, dependable person on staff." A word of praise is far more meaningful to a person if it is tied back to one of his or her qualities such as enthusiasm, intelligence, positive attitude, or integrity than if it's tied to performance results.

We all know that communication is an ongoing process. Praise is all about focusing on the good things that a person does. Instead of focusing only on areas needing improvement, accentuate the positive. Praise motivates people to action and gives them a sense of self-worth. Fran Tarkenton, the legendary NFL football star, puts praise in perspective with his observation that "the person who works well four days out of five ought to be praised four times as often as he's dumped on."

It may take some extra time to deliver meaningful feedback and praise for work done well, but look at it this way: making praise a priority has the power to energize people, change the corporate culture, attract and retain valued workers and ultimately redefine the workplace. A few minutes now can pay big dividends long term.

What we have learned from childhood is to please the person above us by doing it the way they want to get it done, not the way we want it done. You have the board of directors, CEO, COO, and other C levels. Then you have directors, managers, line managers, and then the workers. That's the way it looks. It starts at the top and goes down. Every employee tries to please those above him or her.

Back in the Depression that was a good strategy, because everyone needed a job. Now we live in an era of human rights, and there are a lot of jobs out there. We just aren't going to get it that way. It won't happen. The environment has changed.

The Behavioral Science School

If you draw the hierarchy on a piece of paper and turn it over upside down, and put the workers at the top and then go the other way, now we are trying to please the people who are down below us. What we would be trying to do is serve and acknowledge them in some way so that they want to do their jobs rather than just doing them because we tell them to. What managers would do is go to those people and find out what they need to get their jobs done better. We would do it through acknowledging behaviors and giving them incentives for doing the behaviors we want them to do and eliminating behaviors we don't want them to do. They need recognition, to feel like they belong, and to contribute. We wouldn't be trying to impress the person above us by getting the people below us to do what the upper management wants. We would turn the thing all the way around and try to serve the people who actually do the work and are closest to the customer.

People don't see it that way because they have learned to shout louder, to be more direct, to send longer emails, and to be more reprimanding. They think that's the way to get things done. That works once.

Throughout most of the second half of the 20th century, companies could ignore employees because they could use new technology and new processes to create competitive differentiation. Now that this has all been done and everyone has jumped on this bandwagon, the one thing that is left and has been ignored is the competitiveness you have in your people.

Employees have become even more critical as we have become a knowledge-based society. Almost every job requires knowledge that every employee picks up. Whether you are an accountant or working on an assembly line, every task requires some kind of knowledge. If you talk to people who have been in a job for along time, there are things they know about their job and the company that make them good at their job.

A few years ago a woman was working in the auto department of a large company. She didn't know anything about technology. The company was switching over to all of this new technology, and there was a debate as to her worth for the company.

Then a manager spent time with her and talked with her. She knew every single part and product number off the top of her head. She had been there for 25 years. Over those years the company had been through many product-numbering changes. She knew them all. You could give her an old number from way back when and she could translate that up. That was a very strong resource for both the company's dealers and people internally, because the company had not totally solidified its parts numbering systems. She became someone whom you could go to and give a number and ask what part it was. She could tell you.

Losing her would have cost the company a lot of money and forced it to spend a lot more money to get everything on the same ground faster. Instead, with her there, the company could develop slowly.

That woman showed that there is knowledge in every single employee. If you let good employees go, you create a stronger competitor, and you lose information that isn't in a manual or book. That's why people have become so critical.

Behavioral science can address these issues. It forces managers to look at human capital because they are constantly looking at the system to see what is being measured. It brings it to the top of the awareness reel for everybody involved. It also gives you a way to react. In a lot of cases, people just don't have a way to react. They can ask, "What do I do about this morale problem?" Now there are ways to fix it. More important, a system that builds morale, loyalty, and enthusiasm in employees is preventative medicine, so that reactive modes need never be invoked.

Chapter 3

Behavioral Science Overview

So what is behavioral science?

When you were about four years old, your mother or your father (or both!) told you not to touch the hot stove. You did it anyway. You got burned. You never did it again.

That was behavioral science in action.

The ABCs

Your childhood battle with the stove contained three basic elements, known as the ABCs. Your parents' telling you not to touch the stove was an *Antecedent*, a bit of communication intended to instruct you to do or not do something. Your touching the stove was a *Behavior* – in this case, not the one your parents intended. The pain and blister on your finger were the *Consequences*.

The classic experiments of behavioral science include Pavlov's dogs, who learned to drool at the sound of a bell, and Skinner's boxes, in which rats learned to press levers in exchange for food.

In business an antecedent can be as simple as a memo. The desired behavior might be reorganizing a file cabinet. In most companies employees receive only a single consequence for all the tasks they perform: a periodic raise.

To take full advantage of behavioral science, companies need to consider the ABCs a bit more carefully.

In the age of the internet, antecedents can be personalized, they can recur at regular intervals, and they can be stored on in-house intranets for long-term reference.

Behaviors must be observable – by supervisors, colleagues, or even customers – and they must be measurable, either in the form of done/not done or on a graded scale of how well they were done.

The consequence is the element that is most often ignored. Consequences can be positive or negative, take place immediately or in the future, and be certain or uncertain. If you want to shape behavior, what you do is give the most positive, immediate, and certain consequence to a behavior that you want to keep, and give a negative, immediate, and certain response to a behavior that you want to lose – many in the field refer to this as the PIC-NIC approach. You can look back to how you raised your kids or how you were raised. You shape their behavior by first giving them consequences on an every-time basis. As Skinner showed, over time that creates a habit. You can gradually space out the consequences until you no longer need to give consequences to maintain or extinguish a behavior.

PICs and NICs exist whether you want them or not. For example, the chart below lists five circumstances (antecedents) that might prompt insurance processors to increase the number of claims they handled each day, without regard to quality (a behavior). Whether they maintain this new behavior depends on the strength of the consequences that follow their doing so. Those consequences will be positive or negative, immediate or future, or certain or uncertain.

ANTECEDENTS	CONSEQUENCES	POS/NEG	IMMEDIACY	CERTAINTY
Peers do it that way	Easier to do	Positive	Immediate	Certain
No feedback on individual errors	Takes less time	Positive	Immediate	Certain
Performance appraisal has quantity category	Every claim processed is accepted	Positive	Immediate	Certain
Office has quantity goals and graphs on wall	Get praised by boss for meeting quantity goal	Positive	Immediate	Uncertain
Got chewed out for missing quantity goal	Customers unhappy with company and cancel policy	Negative	Future	Uncertain

As we will see, you will be more successful with PICs than with NICs. You don't use this system to reprimand someone. There is no punishment involved. There is a reward for doing it right, and nothing for doing it wrong. If the boss doesn't respond to or give feedback on a particular behavior, employees are going to stop doing it.

If you press the button on the elevator and it doesn't come, you press it again. The behavior scientists will tell you that if that elevator doesn't come you will keep pushing the button more and more. A behavior that doesn't get results will tend to increase at first, but eventually you will stop doing the behavior. If the elevator still doesn't come, you will stop pushing that button eventually. First you press it once, then you press it twice, then you tap on it. When the elevator doesn't come, you just stop pushing the button if you aren't getting any feedback.

Consequences that are effective for one employee may not be effective for another. A consequence that will motivate a 26-year-old to continue or stop a behavior might be quite different what would effect a 48-year-old, or even for that 26-year-old nine months from now.

The consequences in most companies have been based on a one-size-fits-all model. Once a year, if you are a good boy, they give you a 3-percent raise or give you a bonus. That is a positive thing, but it is future and uncertain. People don't adjust their day-to-day behavior based on that, because there are no certain expectations of that happening.

A point system, in which employees accumulate points and can spend them at any time, on a wide variety of consequences, is more effective. One employee might take more time off to spend vacations with a family he or she wants to raise. For someone else, it might be stock options. For others, it might be dynamic pay: instead of waiting for bonuses at the end of the year, they want to be paid on a flexible basis in every period. This pay period, their results were in the 85th percentile, so the company might pay them in the 85th percentile of their pay grades. Next month might be entirely different; if they have a better or worse month, then that's how they will be paid.

Those are immediate and certain consequences that will prompt people to perform the behaviors that management has decided will promote the corporate strategy.

Consequences are critically important, but remember too that simply spelling out desired behaviors and making a show of observing them will probably improve performance – a phenomenon known as the Hawthorne effect.

In 1927, at a plant in Hawthorne, Illinois, the Western Electric Company conducted studies of how its employees would perform under varied conditions. In one case, a manager looked at his line workers and saw that there wasn't very much lighting and the people weren't spaced very well. He came up with the idea that the company should turn up the lights and space the people out better. He assigned a manager to watch productivity and turned up the lights. Productivity went up. He did it again, and productivity went up again. Then he decided that this was interesting, and wanted to see if that would happen again. He made it very light, which made it very hot, and productivity still went up.

Then he turned the lights down. Productivity went up once again. The results had nothing to do with the lighting; workers were responding because somebody was watching and somebody cared. When the people knew that someone was watching the task, they put that extra effort in.

If you care about and measure behavior, you send a message to the people in the workforce that you do care about it, because you measure it.

Most companies take just the antecedent, leave it that, and assume everything will work out. It's the consequence that truly shapes the behavior, and that's what they don't do.

Potential Uses

You can use behavioral science to promote all three of the critical goals of any company: increased sales, decreased costs, and better customer service.

An airline could improve safety by tracking whether pilots followed the correct procedures and took counsel from the copilots, using nothing more than an observer listening to headset communication. Passengers could use the telephones in the back of the seat in front of them to rate the service they received from flight attendants. (They could even be encouraged to do so with the consequence of bonus frequent flier miles.) Customers at terminals could even get involved. Imagine this:

> Your flight's late, and when you step up to the counter everything goes downhill from there. You had already heard, "The plane will be here in about 15 minutes," three times. Then your seat assignment puts you in the middle seat. "No #@!* way!" you retort, "I'm a Platinum member and my agent has my reservation details." The counterperson responds with a lethargic, "I don't know what to tell you; we're all booked up. Would you mind stepping aside so I can take care of the other customers?"
>
> You walk to the Customer Satisfaction Kiosk and enter the name of the person at the counter and describe the situation. You notice a terminal, gate, and time code are already on the form. There are 4 key areas the electronic satisfaction form asks you to fill out. On a scale of 1-5, with 1 meaning "Yes, very much," and 5 meaning "No, not at all," you answer the questions:
>
> - Did the employee act courteously?
> - Did the employee express concern?
> - Did the employee take responsibility for the problem and offer solutions?
> - Did the employee make eye contact?

You hit "Submit," and another window opens, explaining that your answers have been sent to management and the employee's virtual performance evaluation so the employee can review them. The window also explains that points are awarded for good performance evaluations.

Wow! You are impressed.

What a way to show customers a company cares about their experience!

Consider finance. Insurance companies could want to see how well they handled claims, which can be efficiency related as well as customer service related. Managers could monitor phone calls, and customers could fill out surveys.

Behavioral science can also fit into a business-to-business relationship, in which one business might incent the behavior of another. A wholesaler, for example, could give points to a distributor's employees for pitching their brand rather than another.

The Sales Marketing Network (www.info-now.com) has published an excellent article on these types of incentive programs. The article appears in the box below.

Structuring a Dealer Incentive

Dealer incentive programs differ from other types of incentive programs in one important respect: The recipients are not employed by your company. They either own their own businesses or work for dealers or distributors that resell your products or services. This can complicate the effectiveness of any incentive program.

Most companies sell through some form of a middleman.

Distributors generally take the billing for the products or services they sell to other companies. Dealers, which often buy from distributors or directly from manufacturers, sell products or services directly to consumers or businesses. Agents and independent representatives usually sell to distributors, dealers, or end users and receive a commission from the companies they represent. How your incentive program is structured should reflect the type of middleman you want to motivate and your relationship to the companies involved.

STEP 1: SPECIFY YOUR OBJECTIVES

As with any incentive program, begin by specifying your objectives, if possible in numeric terms. Generally, you should have one primary objective and perhaps one or two others that are related. The primary objective tracks the specific results you want, such as increased sales. The secondary or "process" objectives measure the specific steps participants can take to achieve your primary objective. Some sample primary objectives: Increase sales by 10 percent in the third quarter versus the same period last year; increase the number of dealer salespeople participating in product training programs versus the same period last year; obtain a 20 percent share for a new product in its full year.

STEP 2: DETERMINE WHO – AND WHAT – IS CRITICAL

If your company sells through middlemen, determine which categories or which specific dealers, agents, or distributors are critical to your business. In the consumer business, the role of agents and representatives has declined as the result of growing retail consolidation. Manufacturers no longer need hundreds of representatives when only a few retailers control a large market share. Also, it has become increasingly difficult for consumer-product manufacturers to influence the promotional practices of these giant retailers. Yet, many consumer and business-to-business suppliers still move considerable volume through middlemen, and no incentive program can succeed unless you determine the types of middlemen critical to your success.

In addition, identify precisely what these target audiences can do to help you achieve your objectives: stock more product, participate in marketing or training programs, put up displays, participate in co-op marketing programs, or provide customer databases. Generally speaking, your top 20 percent of dealers contributes the bulk of your business. Thus the objective of incentive programs is not only to get the top performers to stretch a bit further, but to get average performers to increase their participation with your company. Many companies want to target the dealer salespeople who actually present the product to the end user. Dealer principals often resist these programs, fearing that externally sponsored incentive programs motivate their salespeople to act in someone else's best interests. If you want to target salespeople, you must do so in a way that will benefit the principal as well. Some dealers appreciate incentive programs as a way of providing employee perks they can't afford or as an opportunity to provide extra training.

STEP 3: DETERMINE WHAT IS IN IT FOR THEM

Unless you have a tightly controlled group of agents that's dependent on your company – still the case in many industries – you have to compete with many other companies for the attention of your middlemen. Everybody wants the middlemen to focus on their product and is constantly trying to come up with good reasons for them to do so. In the end, most middlemen will do what is best for their customers and for their company, which is not necessarily what is best for you. Savvy suppliers know that they have to offer programs that help middlemen meet their goals of increasing sales and profits. Most middlemen will say that sales and profits are their biggest concerns, but that doesn't mean that adding a percentage point of margin or commission will necessarily produce a significant increase in sales. Dealers and distributors often react more enthusiastically to strategies that help them address fundamental problems, such as fighting competition, improving the training and retention of salespeople, building consumer loyalty, or building sales of a product or service category.

STEP 4: STRUCTURE THE PROGRAM

Most companies want them to stock or sell more of a current

product or participate in co-op marketing programs, but what's the attraction for the middlemen? All of their suppliers want them to stock more products and support it better in the marketplace. Based on your meeting with key distributors or agents, you should have come away with other ways to help them achieve their objectives.

Note: You will get little response unless you set goals that are attainable to a broad portion of your target audience.

By keeping your program simple, you'll boost performance among the middle 60 percent of dealers that can generate the most incremental volume. Finally, make sure that your program does not artificially distort sales by getting middlemen to make big purchases or sales efforts during a program only to do little before or after the qualifying period. Here are various basic incentive program options, which in some cases can be mixed and matched:

• **Open-ended strategy.**
Motivate dealers to stock or sell more by setting goals above the past year's sales quota. These programs are easy to budget, because you base the award on incremental sales over a comparable period. Combine the incentive program with basic training and communications designed to make participants more effective. For new dealers, base the quota on a reasonable estimate of what they should be able to accomplish in a start-up year.

• **Closed-end approach.**
Distribute awards to the top performers in each volume category or region. This is easy to budget but tends to reward top performers who would excel anyway.

• **New product introduction.**
Budget a small amount per unit of your new-product budget for an incentive program designed to get dealers or distributors to increase their commitment to your product. Companies qualify in proportion to their level of commitment. To make this work, you have to provide these companies with an exciting program that will convince them the product will sell through.

- **Plateau programs.**

These reward dealers or distributors in an increasingly significant way for making incremental purchases, say, at 5, 10, or 15 percent above their quota or last year's performance.

The idea is to push people to try harder than they would in a program geared just to an overall increase in sales.

- **Cooperative marketing programs.**

Here you provide extra rewards for dealers for participating in your co-op marketing programs. For instance, they could get bonus points for utilizing co-op dollars, putting up displays, or participating in a training program for salespeople.

- **Product-specific programs.**

Companies offer bonus points for distributors that sell or buy more of a specific product. But you might jeopardize the sale of other products with this approach, so your secondary measures might include a requirement to hit an overall sales target.

- **Database programs.**

Offer dealers and distributors a reward for providing customer names for co-op direct marketing or telephone sales solicitation on behalf of your company's product. This is a good way to collect valuable names in a cause that ultimately should benefit your distribution partners.

- **Training for dealer salespeople.**

Offer credits for special training for salespeople that addresses your dealers' needs, not just your own. This helps your middlemen by improving the caliber of salespeople and helps you communicate with the people who sell your product.

- **Customer-affinity programs.**

Many companies simply invite top distributors and dealers to special meetings that blend training, motivation, and entertainment. Top managers may base selection of attendees on a subjective evaluation.

- **Sales/purchase pushers.**

These promote sales in a particular season to maximize results. If your business is seasonal, you'll want to make sure you profit as much as possible from the potential business in the strongest sales period. Similarly, you can use incentive programs to boost sales in normally slow periods.

STEP 5: DETERMINE YOUR AWARD SYSTEM

Depending on your objectives and audience, you may want to use cash, cooperative marketing dollars, or non-cash awards, such as merchandise, travel, and gift certificates. Mass merchandisers will make their needs known quickly. They probably won't want non-cash awards unless offered as part of a joint promotion for consumers or as assistance in boosting the mass merchandiser's own business objectives, such as improving overall customer service. Smaller business owners and managers, however, often enjoy the benefits of receiving merchandise and travel awards, including the chance to meet with colleagues from other parts of the country. In evaluating your choices, look at what competitors have done and try to ascertain what options will get the most attention. Whatever you do, change it for the following program. Variety is the spice of any ongoing incentive program. Experiment continually and track results.

STEP 6: DEVELOP A TRACKING PLAN

The great advantage of incentive programs, versus other types of marketing efforts, is the ability to track results precisely. All of the structures outlined in Step 4 can be measured clearly, if you track basic sales data. Full-service incentive companies offer tracking programs that not only follow sales activity by dealer or salesperson, but also provide regular updates to the target audience as well as monthly reports to you. Small companies can track a program with a simple spreadsheet program, into which is entered each salesperson's invoices or reports.

STEP 7: DEVELOP YOUR BUDGET

If you structure your budget properly, the program will cost relatively little, unless performance exceeds your quotas or objectives by a wide margin. Most companies don't mind rewarding dealers and distributors for incremental performance. The closed-end program that selects the top performers is the easiest to budget, because you have a predetermined number of winners. However, you risk rewarding your top performers even when the company doesn't achieve its overall goals. The open-ended program is more difficult to budget, since you can't predict precisely how many people will achieve the goal and to what extent.

STEP 8: DECIDE WHO WILL RUN THE PROGRAM

As with any marketing campaign, you'll need someone in-house in charge. Then, establish whether you want to implement the program on your own. The critical issues include administration, databasing, tracking, communications, training, and award fulfillment. Full-service incentive companies handle all these functions, and smaller specialists can take on one or two. Unless you expect billings in the tens of thousands of dollars, larger incentive companies can't help.

STEP 9: WRITE THE RULES

Now that you know the structure and the budget, you have to write the rules that will be incorporated into all of the communications. It's imperative that everybody understands the reward structure in the same way, which means your program, must be simple enough to explain with short sentences on a single page. People don't have time to wade through literature, even when they have a high interest level. The rules should spell out all conditions for participation in the program. Have several people not directly related to your business read the rules to make sure anyone can understand them.

STEP 10: ESTABLISH A COMMUNICATIONS PLAN

Getting the attention of your audience is a challenge, since dealers and distributors receive offers from many suppliers. Make sure your program is easy to understand and filled with benefits to your target audience. Throughout the program, provide participants with useful information to help them succeed with it. Launch the effort with an enrollment kit that asks for basic business address information along with tax identification numbers, when applicable. The kit should also prominently specify the program duration. Since your program should support your marketing objectives, link it as much as possible to the overall marketing push. Develop a theme for the incentive program and try to relate it to your marketing themes. This will help people remember it. In addition to your launch kit, have your salespeople mention the program in their presentations. Hold regional kickoff meetings with dealers and distributors, and send regular updates to all enrollees, providing them with their results to date plus useful information to help them improve performance. How often you communicate depends on the duration of the program.

STEP 11: CONSIDER THE ROLE OF TRAINING
Make sure the dealer salespeople have the knowledge to help you. Many dealers and distributors don't want suppliers having direct contact with their salespeople, so its important to offer training that benefits the principals by improving the overall knowledge of salespeople, not simply information about your product.

STEP 12: LAUNCH AND TRACK THE PROGRAM
Have a formal date for the kick-off and try to stick with it. You will probably want to time the program to coincide with your overall marketing effort. Watch what happens month-by-month by checking your results, and, depending on the results, make adjustments or send out additional information and tips to participants. Remember, you cannot change the rules or qualification levels midstream without annoying your participants and perhaps even violating the law.

STEP 13: CONCLUDE THE PROGRAM
When the qualification period is over, generate reports as quickly as possible to see the results. Waste no time in notifying all participants of their final standing. Many companies stop mailing reminders to dealers or salespeople who don't qualify, on the grounds that people don't like to be reminded of failure. However, you can send out constructive information to such dealers naming the dealers that qualified, along with information about how the non-qualifying dealers could perform better in the future.

STEP 14: DEMONSTRATE YOUR APPRECIATION
No matter what award options you have selected, you should pay close attention to how you present the awards. Much of the

impact is derived from the degree of sincerity coming from the giver. Consider making the award in public, perhaps at a customer council, trade show, national sales meeting, or somewhere else where people can bask in the recognition and know that you appreciate their accomplishments.

STEP 15: EVALUATE AND CHANGE
Look carefully at the results, tracking precisely what happened to sales and other areas that you measured. Isolate the factors that could have affected your program. For the next program, consider changing your measures but continue tracking the old measures as well. This will let you see what happens when your dealers aren't provided incentives, communications, and training on objectives you're attempting to fulfill.

HOW TO AVOID PROGRAM ADDICTION
Many companies that use incentive programs fear that they can become addictive. Here are ways to avoid that:
• **Mix it up.** As in baseball, change your pitches and programs from season to season. Keep dealers and distributors on their toes by surprising them.
• **Change your measures.** Don't always structure your programs the same way, but change them to suit changing objectives and business needs.
• **Juggle incentives with other strategies.** Use programs during some sales periods but not others, so that people, especially competitors, know they are only one part of your marketing arsenal.

Credit: "The Sales Marketing Network at www.info-now.com."

Technology

Technology can be a great help in managing with behavioral science. Automated systems can measure far more behaviors in far greater detail than people can unassisted. Such systems can also ensure that positive and immediate reinforcement takes place. There is something about the human psyche that tends to focus on what is not working and forget to reward and recognize the things that are being done well. The technology creates a structure to measure and recognize the positive action as well as where we are falling short.

Systems also force managers to be objective. When the technology doesn't think on its own, it measures and tracks what we tell it to. It removes bias from the process.

Perhaps most critically, technology brings immediacy. The PIC-NIC analysis tells us that one of the key components to have high impact on reinforcement is the immediacy of the consequence. Technology has the ability to bring reward or recognition swiftly. If employees have workplace access to data on their behavior – through personal computers or handheld devices, for example – they get more involved, because they can see the results more quickly and on a daily basis.

For instance, imagine a salesperson who had a really good call with someone with good results. When this information gets to the manager, there is a consequence associated with the behavior. You can go see it at the end of the day that the person is complimented, rewarded, or recognized for the activity. The desired behavior is reinforced immediately.

In a large company these systems allow you to look collectively at an organization from the enterprise level. You can use the knowledge you gain from one department or segment of your business in another department. You can also create specialized behavior programs for each division – or, theoretically, for every employee – so that everyone can be judged and compensated based on a scale appropriate to their tasks.

For those companies that have freelancers or a dispersed workforce, a company-wide intranet can keep the workforce abreast of what is going on in the company. If a company has customer-service call centers all over the world, it can create pages ranking employees by the number of points they earn. The employees who score well would feel good because they would see their names up there and know that everyone else in the company was seeing them too.

One company used a simple newsletter in a similar fashion to highlight top-performing salespeople spread around the world. When the dealers went to conventions, they sought out those people they had seen frequently in the newsletter, because they felt as if they knew them from reading about them. With an electronic system, such a system can be much more efficient, and done in real time. You can make chat rooms so that these people will have the chance to meet each other and feel like they are part of the group.

Another benefit of automation is that it helps executives figure out whether things like being customer-centric or other goals like that are actually having an impact on the company's earnings. It takes that intangible or invisible asset that you have and it allows you to make it measurable, which then allows you to take your other measurements and show a relationship between the two. You can show through points that you have given frequently for being customer-centric in the past three months. If you look at other measurements such as customer retention in the past three months, and those have gone up as well, then you can see a correlation. In the past that type of comparison would have been hearsay. There would have been a question mark. People might say that the market was better or come up with some other explanation. But today, with automation, you can say with more certainty what activities are critical to your success.

Chapter 4
Setting Goals

As we have seen, behavioral science can help your company achieve nearly any goal. So how do you set the right ones for your organization?

You should limit yourself to those things you see as the three to five goals that will have the most impact on your business. You don't want to try to leverage the approach for every aspect of your corporation. You really need to focus on what are the most important goals that will bring differentiation from competitors or effective change to your strategy. Most people walk into an annual planning process with a list of 20 things they want to achieve. When trying to use behavioral science, it's important that you prioritize and try to pick the top areas.

Beyond that, goals must be specific and measurable. Those things are important to keep in mind. If you just say you want to improve consumer service, you must get far more specific before you can make progress.

Leading vs. Lagging Indicators

Success breeds success. You want to set up a series of goals that are in smaller steps and are attainable so that the end result is success. You want to manage by leading indicators, not lagging indicators. Lagging is setting a goal of selling 10,000 widgets a month, when the highest that anyone has ever sold is 2,000. That may not be possible, and probably won't result in success. If the goal is ridiculous people won't even try to reach it. These long-term, result-oriented targets are lagging indicators because if you're watching only them you won't know until the end of the period whether you've succeeded – and by then it's too late to make adjustments.

A better way is to use leading indicators. Break down the process into observable behaviors that a person needs to perform to sell 10,000 widgets. If you break down these things to a weekly level and then measure and reinforce these behaviors, you'll find success. The end result will be selling the 10,000 widgets, but you don't worry about that end result – you worry about sticking to the process, which will ultimately culminate in success. When Phil Jackson became head coach of the NBA's L.A. Lakers and began to fix the team's offensive process, he didn't start by telling his players to score 100 points a night. He started with where people needed to be and how to distribute the ball. He focused on the process, not on the end result. That's a more predictable and sustainable thing to do.

For example, how do you get a suggestion box to work for your company? If you put up a suggestion box and people submit ideas but never get recognized for doing so, that will lead to extinction of that behavior. You want to recognize them for making that suggestion. It doesn't matter what their ideas are; the behavior you wanted was the suggestion, whether it was good or bad. You are going to get some good ones in there. That's all you want: the behavior, not the results; if cause and effect are linked properly, the results will come.

It may fall to the human resources manager to make sure that senior management understands what is an unrealistic goal. Yet a lot of HR managers can't even tell that themselves, because they may not be knowledgeable enough to sit and tell the VP of operations what is an unrealistic goal. That's why the entire organization must work together on it.

If you keep detailed records of your employees' results, you'll see quickly whether your program is too difficult or too easy. That's because of the defining feature of leading indicators – you can see, before you reach your deadline, how you're progressing on the elements that will promote your ultimate goal. If you see that two weeks into a six-month program, people are halfway to the goal, then you have made it too easy. But even then you wouldn't want to punish them and raise the goal, because that would be a demotivator. What you want to do is create an added bonus beyond the goal. You still give what you promised, but you give further reinforcement for going further.

Many runners approach their sport in a similar fashion. When they go into a race, they have stretch, focused, and minimum goals. They start out at a pace that will help them achieve the focused goals. The external conditions might be good or bad, or training may have been more or less successful than expected, so they will adjust the target as they go. That's a useful approach in business too. As you begin to execute against the goals, if you find if the external conditions, training, or internal preparation enable a more aggressive pace, then you try to get your team to adjust to that.

When you are using a performance program and you are ahead of the game in reaching your goal, it's important to keep yourself ahead rather than taking it easy and sliding by. Here are twelve strategies to help you keep your advantage:

1. Stress to the participants that the program hasn't ended yet and review what needs to be done to keep ahead of schedule.

2. Add another incentive to reach an even higher goal. For example, in a regional real estate office, the goal was 129 closings in a month. If the goal was reached, everyone would enjoy a ¼ percent extra commission as a bonus. By mid-month there were 108 closings. Rather than coast to the goal, the manager felt there was an opportunity for a record month. Although everyone would still receive the additional commission bonus with 129 closings, if the office reached 180 closings, the bonus would be doubled to ½ percent instead of ¼ percent. The office had a record of 187 closings that month!

3. When the goal is especially difficult or represents a deep change in the way things have always been done and you are ahead or on track, stop and have a mini-celebration to re-energize the troops.

4. Recognize individual efforts. Whether the program is group or individually based, recognize the participants with verbal praise or thoughtful gestures such as a handwritten note, public recognition in a meeting, a personal voice-mail message or lunch. Recognize valuable contributions and extra effort.

5. Share the interim results with executives. Because you've drawn attention to the success of the program and the participants, the employees will be more committed to achieving the goals.

6. Run a spontaneous program-within-a-program. For example, the sales incentive program at Excalibur Software rewarded all who increased their sales 10 percent with a weekend vacation. The program had been successful, and almost everyone was ahead. To keep the interest level high and momentum

going, the sales manager pinned a $50 bill to the bulletin board two to three times a week for the sales reps with the highest dollar sales for the day.

7. Expect more and you will get more. A study of school teachers showed that when teachers held high expectations for their students, the elevated expectation alone was enough to cause an increase of 25 points in the students' achievement scores.

8. Foster healthy competition between individuals or groups. "People most strenuously seek to evaluate performance by comparing themselves to others, not by using absolute standards," writes Leon Festinger, a management consultant.

9. Communicate frequently. Everyone loves to hear about progress – and progress fuels further action, which yields results. It all starts with keeping people informed.

10. Build momentum by accumulating small successes. Review what has worked, the achievements and successes. Stress building on these blocks to achieve the greater goal.

11. Let people see clearly that it is in their best interest to promote the company's interest. People are motivated when they understand what's in it for them.

12. Share the vision of success. Articulate what reaching the goal will mean to the individual, the team, and the company.

The only way you can update your goals is by tracking your employees' behaviors and results and providing feedback all the time, just as runners track every mile marker and constantly assess whether they are breathing too hard and how their legs feel. You must constantly evaluate whether the behaviors you have selected are effective and gaining traction with the customers or affecting a change in your culture or achieving any other goal you have in mind. If the behaviors are not bringing the intermediate results you expected, then you need to make adjustments there.

There is one caution here. If you want to evaluate trends, you need to keep your metrics the same long enough to track performance. You can change your goals, extend them, change the consequence-approval process, budget, or behaviors that make up the program. You have a lot of flexibility. But you need to think through what will happen to your data before you make those changes.

In addition to being attainable, goals should be short- rather than long-term. Remember the PIC-NIC! A long-term goal of increasing sales by 20 percent by the end of the year to get a bonus may be positive, but it is not immediate. It is way out in the future and is not certain. Even if you say you are going to give them a 20 percent bonus, the employee doesn't really know if the company is going to be there, or if they are definitely going to get what you promised. Employees are also liable to procrastinate, deciding that they'll do most of the work after a vacation, when they think they'll be more relaxed.

But if you say to them that instead of a long-term goal of meeting dollars and sales, they need to make 3 percent more calls in one week, they can focus in on that. You can tell them that if they do that, you are going to take care of them on that thing. If they are able to do this, you are going to give them a thousand points.

With the short-term approach, you can get a lot more than the 20 percent increase at the end of the year.

You're using a positive, immediate, and certain consequence to encourage a behavior that promotes that goal.

You can have different goals for different departments or even for different individuals. Regardless of what your goals are, any program based on behavioral science that treats each employee individually will promote an important by-product for any company: employee retention.

At my company, for example, we have someone who is getting her MBA. She is in a coordinator position, and probably could get a better position somewhere else. But this is an exciting environment, and we give her a lot of responsibility and feedback. She is interested in marketing, so we make sure she is constantly being educated on marketing and the different facets of it. Those are the positive consequences she receives for performing the duties we assign her. That will keep her here for a while. In my mind that sort of tailored reward is what a manager should be providing. The people are just going to leave and be unsatisfied if they don't like their jobs and how they are being reinforced for performing them.

A point-based consequence system also encourages employees to remain with your company. Like stock options, the points become more valuable the longer employees hold onto them. The system still works as an encouragement to short-timers, however, because the consequences come quickly and certainly. They don't have to wait for annual rewards but can spend their points whenever they like.

Nearly any behavioral-science based program will also automatically help newly-minted managers adjust to their responsibilities. Many new managers micromanage.

An organized system of incentives will encourage them to give up some of their responsibilities, because it will give them a formal process for staying involved. They won't need to rely on their inexperienced judgment to decide when to look over their employees' shoulders.

Once top executives have goals in mind, they can begin to set up a program. If the system will be computerized, the first step is to get all the employees loaded to represent the organizational hierarchy. Once the employees are in place, depending on how the company wants to administrate the program, a manager could have the authority to set up specific elements themselves or they may work with someone who is an expert at designing or setting up programs.

Initially managers will probably go to a project administrator who will load the program. Over time the managers will learn to run the system themselves.

The appointment of an initial program administrator is a critical component in the implementation of a reward program. The administrator is the change agent and becomes the manager of motivation in a reward or incentive program. He or she is in charge of planning the program, tracking the program, making any necessary adjustments, and communicating the status and ultimately the results of the program.

Typically, the administrator is a manager. It is the central role of management to create an environment in which motivated people can flourish. The administrator in a comprehensive reward program needs to be a leader, manager, coach, trainer, teacher, and cheerleader simultaneously. He or she leads and manages by having the answers to employees' questions and by setting an example. He or she coaches, trains, and teaches by showing and reinforcing the correct behavior, supplying tips on improvement, and delivering thoughtful criticism and praise when needed. The administrator is aware that cheerleading is important when things get done. It's important to remember that what is reinforced gets repeated.

A good administrator:

- must have a positive, can-do, this-will-work attitude,
- should not be a participant,
- should have close contact with the participants and know what motivates them,
- should be able to communicate both to upper management regarding the program status and to participants,
- must be able to anticipate and avoid problems,
- should be fair and impartial,
- should be available,
- should have excellent follow-through skills,
- must pay attention to detail, and
- should be able to deliver thoughtful, constructive criticism when necessary.

Once the software is in place and someone has been selected to operate it, a company must determine what behaviors to promote. No matter what goals you have chosen, you will be able to find underlying behaviors. Behavior influences everything that happens in a company.

The Springfield Gazette – A Story of Behavioral Science in Business
Part 1

The top business-side executives of *The Springfield Gazette* gathered in the conference room for the daily 8:30 meeting, many of them with copies of that morning's paper under their arms.

"Let's get right to it," Publisher Bill Haskins said, once everyone was seated. "With the economy stalling the way it is, our ad revenues are way down. Our newsstand sales are down. Subscriptions are doing okay, but that's probably only because it hasn't occurred to readers to save money by canceling. I've been reading about behavioral science, and I think we can use it to stay afloat, and maybe even to make some improvements."

Haskins paused as the vice presidents sitting around the conference table settled in for what they could already tell would be a longer meeting than usual.

"Now, I know what you're thinking," the publisher said, shooting a glare in the direction of the vice president for marketing, who had let loose a clearly audible sigh. "We've tried a few of these hot management strategies before, but this one will be different. It really makes a lot of sense. The first thing we need to do is come up with some goals. What do we want to do here at the Gazette?"

"Make more money," the treasurer replied immediately. Everyone, including the publisher, laughed.

"Yes, but how do we make more money?" Haskins asked.

The executives looked at each other uncertainly.

"We need to sell more ads?" suggested Marsha Jones, the director of advertising sales.

"That's better," Haskins said. "Selling ad space brings in 60 percent of our revenues, so that's a good place to start. But let's get more specific. How many more ads?"

"Let's double our money over the next three years."

Everyone turned to Nathaniel Bixby. He was known around the water cooler – sarcastically – as Big Idea Bixby, because he had a habit of coming up with grand schemes like this one. Haskins knew just how to handle him.

"That would certainly be great, Nathaniel," he said. "But let's try to think a little more short-term. How about a 12 percent increase in sales revenue over the next six months? Do you think we can do that, Marsha?"

"In this economy I'm not so sure. But maybe."

"I don't want us to aim so high that we miss," Haskins said. "How about 10 percent, and we'll start off slow, looking for just one percent in the first month."

Jones nodded, and the publisher in turn nodded to his assistant, who wrote the short- and long-term targets on a whiteboard, under the heading "Goal 1."

"What else can we do?" Haskins asked the group.

The executive responsible for single-issue sales, Jim Watts, raised his hand.

"I'd certainly like to do something about newsstand sales, but they really depend on the people who run the newsstands. Once we drop off the bundle in the morning, sales are out of our hands."

Haskins nodded.

"That's okay, we'll get the shopkeepers involved in this too. What kind of target did you have in mind?"

"Well, I'm not sure," Watts said, turning a bit red and glancing around at his colleagues. Conventional wisdom said that single-issue sales depended on what was on the front page on a given day, whether the local minor league ballclub had won or lost, and even on the weather – commuters tended to skip their stop at the convenience store if it was raining between 7 and 9 a.m. All of this meant that Watts wasn't used to the spotlight during these strategy sessions. He hesitated, then continued.

"If you really think we can get help from the newsstand operators, I think we might be able to get sales up three percent over six months. Unless the Spiders lose the day before you measure, or there's a storm, or – "

"Don't worry, we'll use a three-day sales average to get a fair measure," Haskins said. "And you don't sound too confident about three percent; let's go with two instead. We'll come up with some intermediate targets in a minute."

The publisher's assistant added Goal 2 to the whiteboard.

"What else can we do?"

"Speaking of the Spiders, I think they should get more coverage," said Jones, the ad exec. "And what about improving the color on the front page? It's been looking pretty flat lately."

Haskins shook his head.

"Those are good points, but they're a little narrow," he said. "Let's come up with one more goal that will really have an effect on the bottom line."

"We can always try a subscription drive, but I don't know how that will play with people getting laid off and gas prices going up and everything else," said Rachel West, head of the subscriptions department.

"We'll sell the paper as an investment," said Watts, apparently encouraged by his success earlier in the meeting. "If you read us, you'll be able to anticipate the next spike in gas prices, and you'll have a better sense of how secure your job is. And of course we've got classifieds in case you get laid off. Really, people need newspapers now more than ever!"

"Excellent!" Haskins nearly shouted. "That's just the sort of approach we'll need to use. But let's keep this goal modest. We'll try to increase the number of subscribers by two percent in six months."

"You're the boss," West said. "But what does any of this have to do with behavioral science?"

The publisher smiled as his assistant added the final goal to the whiteboard behind him.

"Ah, that's the next step," he said. "The behavioral science comes in paying attention to behaviors, of course. These goals are great, but now that we've got them we won't worry about them too much. We're going to focus on what our people need to do to achieve them."

Chapter 5

Pinpointing Key Behaviors

The people in senior management create a strategy of being customer-centric and email it to everyone in the company. What does that mean for the forklift driver? Or for anyone else in the organization?

The first step toward finding the behaviors that will promote the chosen goals is to look at the different employee populations that are involved in reaching those goals. If a goal was to improve customer service, and I had a telephone-order catalog service, I would think through all the different people or roles that get involved in the actual delivery of that service. I would think about what specific behaviors would help improve the perception of the delivery of customer service. That's the intellectual process.

The approach loses its impact if you try to include every relevant behavior. That dilutes the value of it. So, at one company I worked with we began with 60 behaviors that drove the bottom line. The executives knew, however, that 80 percent of their difficulties were in just nine areas. So we focused on those. Then once in a while we would swap a different behavior in.

In their customer-service call centers, for example, we focused on one issue: service reps' asking for permission to look at customer records. They knew that by law you have to ask the person you are talking to if you can look at their records. They knew if they didn't do that, they couldn't offer to sell them caller ID. The salespeople must look at the records to see if that person has it, if that person pays his or her bills – in short, if it is even worth it to give it to them.

The reps could simply ask, "Is it OK if I look at your records?" Customers would probably ask why, and the reps would say, "Because I want to sell you something."

The customers don't want anything, so they would decline. We noticed that the service reps are reluctant to ask this question because they get shut down so much.

So we set up a system in which reps receive 1,000 points every time they ask that question. Now, since the reps are asking it all the time to earn the points, they figure out how to ask it to match it to their own personality and how to adjust to the caller on the line. If they asked in a whole different way, then the customer might be more willing to let them look at the records. Through doing this hundreds of times, the reps would figure out how to ask the question right.

That same company was also interested in call time. They were timing the service reps and rewarding them based on fast service. Yet at the same time, through other initiatives, the company was trying to be customer-centric. The goals conflicted, because if you have reps worrying about how long they are on the phone with a customer, they are more likely to just blow them off. By reinforcing a shortened call cycle, the company was upsetting customers. They actually had one metric working against another one. They were working against their ultimate goal. This is very common for companies.

By bringing all of the company's behavior-based initiatives together in one program, we could see the conflict very quickly. Such programs also quickly reveal which initiatives don't affect the bottom line. If we see something doesn't have any impact, that's a warning sign that you are measuring and rewarding the wrong things. When a company tries to implement something that has to do with human effort, and managers are not measuring it, then they actually may be rewarding and reaffirming the wrong behaviors and activities, and they may not even realize it. This could go on for years.

Combining company strategy with an incentive program – with compensation, essentially – can transform human resources. All the administration that HR execs had to do in the past when it came to evaluation, recognition, rewards, and reinforcement is centralized and requires fewer people to operate. The manual part of the job is now much more automated and systemized.

At the same time, behavioral science allows human resources executives to become strategic leaders of their organizations. The folks in HR suddenly gain the tools to identify how an individual's performance maps right back up to senior management strategy. That has always been the big gap for human resources. Everything was done in loose terms – saying the company needed "increased loyalty and retention." What does that really mean? Systematic use of behavioral science helps you identify what problems you are having, identify the solutions, and find the way to recognize and evaluate employees for their efforts so that they will want to stay around and do a better job.

You can find critical behaviors in all kinds of employees in all kinds of companies:

> In a service or manufacturing environment where people do repetitive work, like an assembly line, a goal might be to improve the quality of the assembly of the product and reduce defects in parts or products. There are all these people assembling cars on a frame – if something doesn't quite fit, they shouldn't be afraid to

stop the line and fix it, and they should be rewarded, not punished, for that. An assembly line like that would work. (A manager could enter observations into a desktop computer or into a handheld device that he or she carried while walking up and down the line.)

On that same assembly line, if you want to increase speed, you reward employees for taking advantage of periods in a wait mode to go to where the bottleneck in the line is to help remove that bottleneck, and then returning to their stations.

In a sales organization, you might want to improve the quality of reps' sales process. Employees could be encouraged to follow a particular pitch script, to create leads for themselves, to follow up on leads in a certain time, and to get customer data that is necessary for follow-up.

In any company, a senior executive might not be as visible among the employees as she should be. You could set up a system in which she is reinforced for doing that. (You would probably have to give her a lot more points or recognition than people lower in the hierarchy. Her recognition might be different.)

In a plant where safety is a concern, you might be inclined to reward a group of employees that hasn't had any accidents for six months. The problem with this is, what behavior did you just incentivize? You are incentivizng people not to report accidents. If I report my accident, there are 85 people in the plant who aren't going to get those extra bonus points you promised if no one in the plant got into an accident. Now the managers have no way of knowing what real safety is. Instead they should focus on whether employees are wearing the right equipment or following the right procedures, such as lifting materials using the right form.

In a store where you want your salespeople to focus on customers, you might remind your employees that they can pay attention to the customers only while talking to them. So you prize talking to customers over all other behavior. If you want your reps to sell products in packages instead of individually, or to place orders over the Internet rather than over the phone, you set up incentives for those behaviors. If you want your dealers to forecast their sales, you teach them how to do it and start providing them with points and recognition for supplying you with three months' worth of forecasted sales.

Alternatively, you might want in-store salespeople to focus on making pitches. Instead of having a bunch of employees sitting around getting paid an hourly wage, or paying them for selling, pay them for how many times they turn the tip and actually perform a demonstration with the product.

All companies train employees, and here too you can use behavioral science. When employees come in and sign up for training, they get rewarded, recognized, or reinforced. Then they might be reinforced at the end when they take an exam. The important part would be not to reward them for a high grade, but for the behavior of taking a course, because that's what you want them to do.

If it's an online training, you can ensure people aren't just clicking through the pages because you can include interactivity all along the way. One quarter of the way through, you include some sort of test. You can't be sure that it isn't the employee's brother doing the course online, but at least you know that somebody has done it.

You might even include a whole range of courses that employees can complete at home. You could mix in "soft training," such as lessons on activities that they might want to do with their kids, like making paper airplanes. Employees don't get rewarded for that, but it hooks into the system and you can tell they took that lesson. It's a morale issue. It's the whole person, not just the person at work. You are encouraging them to spend time at home with their families and that builds the value system. You give them something they can use.

From a manager's perspective, the most important thing is that you want to make sure that you are translating your corporate goals into behaviors that have meaning to the people that you are communicating with.

From the employees' perspective, this method creates better understanding. The idea that they are part of something bigger and not just viewed as a cog in the machine is important. When they start understanding senior management's goals, and why they want you to do these things this way, then they are going to feel like they are a part of something bigger.

For that reason you often want to share top performers' results with the whole company. But if you are using a ranking system, you need to compare employees to others in similar positions. Within groups, everyone should be judged against the same standard.

The book *Unlock Behavior, Unleash Profits*, by Leslie Braksick, (New York: McCraw-Hill Companies, Inc., 2000) describes a tool to help define behaviors objectively, called the NORMS of objectivity. The acronym stands for: not an interpretation, observable, reliable, measurable, and specific:

> *Not an Interpretation* – The behaviors should be stated objectively, not subjectively, so they are based on clear facts rather than personal feelings, opinions, and biases.
>
> *Observable* – The behaviors should be observable. An observable behavior can be observed directly through one's senses.
>
> *Reliable* – The behaviors should be reliable. A reliable behavior is one that two or more people agree they observed. This is also a good test of objectivity.
>
> *Measurable* – The behaviors should be described in a measurable way, so companies can accurately assess the progress being made.
>
> *Specific* – The behaviors should be described very specifically, so they can be better communicated and understood.

All of the NORMS criteria should be met for a pinpointed behavior to be described well.

If goals – and therefore the required behaviors – expand, the rewards or reinforcements should grow as well. If management said you had to make twice as many phone calls each day, period, you could be quite demotivated. You might start looking for other jobs unless they came up and told you that for that effort they will give you extra money or points. They would have to find out what would motivate you.

The theory there is that if you have happy employees, they are going to give more, emanate that positive vibe, that air of confidence, and that winner mentality that people intuitively pick up when they are thinking about joining a company, buying from a company or having an affiliation with a company. When you have happy employees projecting that image, it has that resonance around external audiences. People want to be around winners, they want to be around confident, positive people. Conversely, sour, unhappy, disengaged people are going to send that message out and people will want to stay clear of them.

Observing Behaviors

By definition, a behavior is something that is observable. There are, however, behaviors that are more easily observed than others. An example would be if people are dealing with customers, it is easy to observe whether they use a certain kind of phrase during that interaction, such as saying their names or promoting a new product. Behaviors that are more difficult to observe often appear when the work environment requires someone work one-on-one. You can't have an observer in the room, so managers would have to use other technologies to gain that information. An example of that would be when you were on a phone conference with a service representative at a call center. Three other people are listening in on a call. While it may sound too good to be true, I don't know that there really is a behavior that isn't a good candidate for observation.

To record those behaviors, the evaluation is either qualitative or quantitative. A quantitative evaluation is made when a completed behavior is graded on a scale, say from one to 10. A qualitative evaluation is a simple yes or no – it was either done or not done.

There are three basic ways for managers to collect observations of employees' behaviors.

1. The first is literally direct observation. In the case of a forklift driver, a manager can simply watch the way that he stacks the boxes, where he stacks them, and in what time frame. Those three different measures have an effect on the corporate strategy of being customer-centric: if he wasn't stacking the boxes carefully, then they would topple over and damage the product. If he wasn't putting the boxes in the right place or time frame, that would delay shipping.

2. Then you have nomination. That's where you create a program in which peers can nominate peers for behaviors or activities or values that align with the company strategy. Consider, for example, an

amusement park that places a high value on keeping its grounds neat and clean as a form of customer service. Imagine an executive of the company that owns the park giving a tour. If he saw a scrap of paper on the ground, he might pick it up and put in his pocket, suit and tie and all.

In that case, if a ride operator saw him do that, the ride operator would have the ability to nominate him for a reward because he is exhibiting customer-centric behavior that is valued by the company. The executive is "getting caught" doing something right. The operator would give a description of what he did: he ran out of his way when he was with a visitor, and he is not the janitor by any means. That would be sent off, and a boss could approve or reject the nomination. If it's approved, the boss will give the executive an allotted number of points. That would be emailed to him or presented in public with a certificate. If the system is automated, every time he checked in he would see how he earned these various awards for being customer-centric. It acts as a great reinforcer for his behavior.

Nominations are a peer-to-peer system, which can be very strong in changing an environment very quickly. If you get everybody being rewarded for exhibiting behavior, it's very healthy. A boss can't be observing everything at the same time. If you create a peer-to-peer environment, you get your whole organization thinking that way. They know that they have people looking at them through, in this case, customer-service eyes.

A slight variation of the nomination system would be to assign observation duty randomly to various members of the staff. Employees know there is a mystery observer out there, but they don't know who it is. That way, one person doesn't get stuck with the load of making those observations, and you receive the positive lift from the Hawthorne effect.

A further variation, which is necessary in some situations, is self-nomination. A lot of consulting organizations do that, because consultants work on their own. They are out there working with the client, and nobody is around to give them a pat on the back. The boss is based in another city. Self-nominations must go through an approval process, which might involve interviews with customers. The managers need to make sure people aren't just making things up.

Recently, many observers of the business world have been predicting that in the future, human capital management will be "the responsibility of each employee in every role in the organization" (The Gartner Group, Human Capital Management: Out of the Hands of HR, February 22, 2000.). Behavioral science allows the HR person or senior management to create the standard of what needs to be measured and how a company should be treating people, and how a program would award recognition. The program then becomes a tutor to all the managers and supervisors. In the case of a nomination-based, peer-to-peer program it can also become a tutor to the employees. The company strategy, which involves the human element, can be quickly proliferated because everyone knows what defines success in their world and gets immediately reinforced for behaving in that manner.

3. The final method of collecting observations is more automated. If you are a salesperson, for example, you are probably already using a computer system to keep track of your contacts and sales, and perhaps even of your telephone script. The data already being collected can easily be combined with an incentive system. Then, any time you fill in a field in an application, there are triggers being sent to record what is being done. For example, the screen would flash and say that you have filled in the customer notes field. That trigger can be grabbed. It would be a yes-or-no evaluation. Yes, this salesperson filled in this field. That trigger is then sent to managers, who can apply recognition. That is then sent back to you and you are reinforced for inputting this data that is helping the company succeed.

In environments where people are separating product at a plant, or entering data into a database, these systems are particularly effective because these jobs are repetitive and are tough to do. Workers feel as if there is no chance for recognition because they are doing the same thing that a hundred other people are doing. How can they stand out? This system gives them a way.

At the same time, it really can be used across the board from piece work to blue collar and white collar work. You can even use this for senior management so they can evaluate themselves. A lot of senior managers need help with different things, but who can they go to? If you set up the system correctly, you have the senior manager being rewarded for behaviors too. If you are paying someone $300,000 a year, you hope that the person is doing something that benefits the company in a strategic way. Most CEO's can't guarantee that a person is doing that on a regular basis. For senior management, the behavior might be something as simple as talking to people. You would get the observation from those people. Every time a staffer has a good interaction with the boss, that staffer could nominate him or her for a reward. I would have the employees rate the conversations they have had with the person. Or employees would rate the meetings the boss had. Every meeting would be followed by an email to everyone present with certain questions, depending on what you are trying to reinforce with that particular person. For example, did she let you speak? Was she overbearing? Did she have her mind made up about decisions beforehand? She would be reinforced, and if you measure those same attitudes or metrics over a given period of time, she will start to see a trend developing as to what she need to work on. At the same time, you end up developing an engaged and loyal workforce that feels confident in the company. The system would have to be anonymous, of course, but there's no reason it couldn't work.

Behavior is behavior. It is observable and the science and technology can promote it or extinguish it. It ranges from safety and security to selling. You can make people more efficient, more externally focused, or more internally focused, and you can retain the best employees that some companies are having trouble keeping.

The only area in which the approach gets more complex is when people are doing on-demand and ad hoc behavior, which is done on a non-repetitive basis. An example would be managers' being measured on how well they are leading. One day they are dealing with a performance issue, the next day they are trying to recruit, and the next day they are trying to build a business plan. How can each of these things be rated? It can be done, but it requires careful planning.

Technology

One of the reasons that no one ever monitored employee behavior on such a large scale before is that keeping track of all this is difficult, and deciding what consequences to give people is also difficult. But with recent advances in technology, the administration doesn't need to be complex at all. Now you can have a record of all these different performance evaluations that you are recognizing people for. You also have a way to show that you are aligned with corporate strategy. You can look at a report and see what are the activities and behaviors that someone is partaking in on a regular basis, and how do those fit with your overall goals. You can look at a report that shows trends of how well a person is performing. You can see which behaviors have a pejorative effect upon other behaviors.

With that information in hand, you can move beyond keeping track of customers and beyond even keeping track of employees, and combine the two. You can create metadata, information about the information, about how one plays into the other. Now you can see how your employees are contributing to your bottom line.

As you monitor behaviors and results over time, you can adjust long-term goals and predictions accordingly. As the data come in you can see how they compare to your projections, and you can make an assessment as to whether you are exceeding or falling short of your expectations.

That ability for adjustment marks the difference between using leading and lagging indicators. If you have the right relationship between cause and effect – meaning that you have the right process and the right steps to achieve end results – then early on, if you are measuring and tracking the steps in the process, you can be assured that the end result will be there. Because the behaviors happen before the results – they lead – you see them first. But if you are focused solely on the results – which lag behind the rest of your activities – you know that you hit or missed your target only after you have done so.

If you do believe in cause and effect, that certain behaviors will produce certain results, then behavioral science allows you to do this. Here's a great example. Public companies are noted for their CEO or CFO having to get up at the beginning of the new quarter to report on earnings from the last quarter. Any time there is a surprise in earnings, the stock takes a huge tumble and there is an embarrassment. If you are running your companies with leading indicators, you can more readily assure yourself that you are going to hit the bottom line. You can tell analysts you are definitely going to make earnings and establish a confidence and predictability that rewards your stock.

If you measure with lagging indicators, you don't necessarily know how you are going to get the number, but you are assuring stockholders you are going to get it. You might make it or you might not. In the end if you didn't, it's too late to adjust. Companies get around this now with huge hedges. They have reserve funds. When times are good, they don't report as much of the earnings and keep them in reserve, so that if they miss down the road they can release those earnings to cover the difference. Wouldn't it be wonderful not to do any of this?

Shortening the time frame in which you reward behavior, then, not only shortens the time frame of being able to recognize someone, but it also shortens the time frame of getting an advance look at your results. It gives you more chances to see how department heads are giving out praise or points, to see what the affect is on return on investment. You can make a subjective or objective evaluation of morale and of synergy between strategic objectives and behavior within your company. If you do this on a weekly or even daily basis, you are going to see results and be able to see whether the steps being taken by the organization are going to lead to the results you're after that much faster.

If you get all the managers to measure their people every third day on three things they do that you know aligns with your corporate strategy of increasing sales, then you can find out fairly quickly by looking at the trend reports how many people are actually achieving these three performance indicators and how many aren't. If 30 percent of the group is not reaching these indicators 70 percent of the time, then you know you are not going to achieve your corporate strategy by the end of the year, and that you are going to have to start making adjustments.

Measurement gives clear feedback to participants and managers. When constructing a measurement system, some pitfalls to avoid are

- measuring the wrong activity,
- trying to measure too many activities,
- changing the measurement system mid-stream,
- measuring irrelevant activities,
- using unrealistic goals and measures,
- using rigid and inflexible measurement systems,
- including irrelevant modifiers, which would not make the system fair and understandable,
- failing to describe the measure or adequately quantify it,
- failing to make sure numbers are normalized if needed, and
- failing to identify method of measurement as objective or subjective.

All of this puts a very new spin on the job of a middle manager. Isn't his primary task to spur his employees to complete the right tasks – that is, to take care of human resources? There shouldn't be a department called HR in the administrative sense that it exists now; those duties should be the job of the guy in the trenches. It's that same transformation that took place in the 1980s and early 1990s, when the job of the quality manager was distributed throughout entire organizations, except far more cogent. If you have interactions with or responsibility for human beings in your enterprise, you better know what you are doing and understand consequences and behaviors, because you are leading people.

According to a February 2001 report by CIBC World Markets, U.S. companies spend nearly $1,500 per employee on human resources. The vast majority of those dollars are spent on administration, with only a few left over for strategy. With behavioral science, will there be no HR? No, just like there are quality departments today, there will be a function called HR, but it will be far smaller and far more interested in strategy.

Sharing Data With Employees

Leaving aside the rewards employees will receive for doing well, in most behavioral science–based systems they will be able to see the simple data of what they are doing, good or bad. The data might be made available via employees' personal, password-protected portions of an intranet. In a program in which managers observe behaviors, the observations could be available to the employees instantly, assuming managers enter the data directly into the system. (The translation is even faster in a program in which the observations are automated, such as a call center in which sales reps enter information into a computer.) With a telephone or wireless interface the data could also be available right away, though employees of course would see it only when they checked into the system. If managers begin with a paper record, the only delay would be the one before the paper records are computerized.

If a manager needs to approve a nomination, to make sure favoritism isn't going on, then the system would refer observations to the manager first for approval, and then disseminate it for consequences and updates to the employees.

Another variation might be that when managers enter observations into the computer, they have the opportunity to put them in a pending state. This would allow them to come back and review them. Once they have completed them and indicate they're done, the system immediately sends a message to the employee that he or she has a new observation. It is also still available for the supervisor or manager to see.

Quick turnaround is especially important in automated systems, in which employees are effectively observing themselves. Salespeople used to be able to pick up the phone and call headquarters and say they spoke with XYZ Company, and they will have three orders. They had a secretary doing all of this data input for them. Now we are asking them to do this themselves. Now they have taken on a second job in their minds. Not only do they have to sell the product, they have to be the secretary for it too. You can talk to them and tell them that this is a benefit to them because over time the information they are inputting will help them see trends in their own work and provide better service or product to the customer. The problem is that they will not experience a benefit from the data until it starts to be a good, robust concentration of information. So the data has to be available quickly. You might even create another award system to encourage people to take part in the program that is your true focus.

While overkill is a more significant problem in the area of actual rewards, it can cause difficulties in simple observation as well. In many cases employees get observations no more than once a week. You want it to be pretty random, with constant positive reinforcement early on but conditioning the behavior over time such that eventually it becomes a habit or an ingrained skill, requiring at first only random and ultimately no reinforcement.

The data itself is measured, tracked, recorded, and accumulated so that you can do trend charting. So you could see on a quantitative basis how you did last month, or on any period versus how you did in another period. Employees can also compare themselves to peers to see how they rank. The system could line teams up against each other, like the baseball standings in your morning newspaper.

In addition to receiving a score, employees and teams should be able to see what contributed to the score – these were four behaviors that the company wanted, these were the observations, and these were the comments. So as a result you can give both the quantitative and qualitative forms of feedback on a real-time basis.

Who within the company should have access to different pieces of data? The technology can do whatever you like. The recommended approach would be that the data could be made available to the employee and his or her supervisor. In terms of comparison data, you adhere to a population of similar workers. If you are ranking, employees might see how well they are doing against others in similar jobs. In a sales organization, for example, employees might see a historical record displaying how everyone ranked in each week or month and exactly what their numbers were. There are some cultures that are used to displaying everybody's score for everyone's viewing. In other cultures, though, employees may be shocked at such bluntness. You need to be aware of what will work in your organization.

Managers should have access to data on their own performance but also to that on their team's. When they delve into their team data, they can go to any individual and look at activity there, or look at an aggregate roll-up of all the activity.

In most companies a manager will tell people to perform a task but will have no idea how well or how often they are actually doing it. With behavioral science you are measuring tactical steps toward achieving the goals. You can find out quickly if the goals are on track to be met because you are reinforcing the steps that lead to the attainment of the goals. If both the observations and the rewards are automated, managers can look at those reports and see if workers are being reinforced or not. If they are not, then something is being left to chance. In the same way, top executives can watch to ensure that middle managers are rewarding their staff. The system acts as a flag for the top guys if the chain of reinforcement is breaking anywhere throughout the organization.

Before any of this can work, however, employees have to be told what's important to the organization.

The Springfield Gazette
Part 2

Bill Haskins began to tell his employees about the principles of applying behavioral science to business.

"The key," the publisher said, "is to focus on the behavior that you need from your employees – not just the results you expect that behavior to lead to. A marathon runner doesn't spend the whole race thinking about how he wants to knock 20 minutes off his time. He focuses on improving his speed for each mile by 55 seconds or a minute. He checks his watch at every mile marker to see how he's doing."

"But our employees aren't runners," said Nathaniel "Big Idea" Bixby. "They know how to focus on long-term goals."

"They might know how to, intellectually," Haskins replied, "but not many people are truly motivated by a vision of the future, way off in the distance. It's too easy to put the work off until tomorrow. If at the end of this meeting I tell you that I'll be distributing doughnuts in five minutes, you'll be sure to stick around for those five minutes, won't you? Immediate consequences have real effects."

"So how do we apply this to our goals?" asked Rachel West, vice president for subscriptions, nodding toward the conference room's whiteboard. The three goals were written neatly in red:

1. Raise ad revenue by one percent in one month and by 10 percent in six months.
2. Raise newsstand sales by two percent in six months.
3. Increase subscriptions by two percent in six months.

Haskins explained that the group would consider each goal one at a time, determining what employees would have to do to help the company achieve them.

"What do our sales reps need to do to increase revenue?" he asked.

"All kinds of things!" replied Marsha Jones, the director of advertising sales. "They need to maintain current advertisers, they need to convert small-ad accounts into big-ad accounts, they need to find new advertisers, they need to reduce the cost of producing ads – the list is endless!"

"Don't worry, we're going to pick out five or six key items. Those are good issues, but think about the specific actions the reps need to take on a daily basis."

Jones thought for a few moments, occasionally scratching out notes on a pad in front of her. The other executives watched, relieved that they didn't have to go first.

"Okay, how's this:" Jones said, reading from her pad: "One, reps need to check in with existing advertisers to ensure that they're not having any problems. Two, before leaving the office at night reps need to check with the composers who paste up the paper to make sure that all the ads that are supposed to be in the next day's paper will really be there. Three, when talking to existing small-ad advertisers, sales reps need to discuss the benefits of buying larger ads. Four, when opening new accounts, they need to advise customers to create the ads themselves – even though we charge extra for custom work, our profit margin is better if the customers just give us completed ads. Five, reps need to call businesses that advertisewith our competitors and talk up the *Gazette*."

"Perfect," said Haskins. "Can you check whether they're doing each of those things, either every day or with spot checks?"

"Well, we monitor some of the reps' phone calls to advertisers already, just to keep an eye on things. The monitors could have a list of the things reps are supposed to say and check them off. They wouldn't listen to every phone call, but it would be enough to keep people honest. The bit about going to the paste-up room could be more formal – we could put a sign-in list down there, and I could pick it up every morning to see whose names were on it and whose weren't. Then I could yell at whoever wasn't doing the right thing."

"No, no, there won't be any yelling," Haskins said. "We'll get to consequences in a few minutes. But first let's look at the behaviors that are related to our other goals."

"The behaviors related to newsstand sales are all about the newsstand operators," said Jim Watts, who was responsible for single-issues sales.

Haskins smiled.

"I know – you told us that before," he said. "Pretend for a minute that the newsstand operators work for you. What would you tell them to do to increase sales?"

"I'd want them to place the *Gazette* more prominently than the *Daily Record*," Watts said. "I'd want them to hang a full front page from the side of their stands, so people passing by could see both above and below the fold. I'd want them to ask people who buy coffee or magazines if they'd like to buy a *Gazette* too. That would be really great. I could check on them easily enough, just by walking by every day and by trying to buy something once in a while. But I don't know why they should care whether I'm happy."

"We'll get there in a minute. Did you write those behaviors down?"

Watts shrugged and wrote down the three points.

"I guess I'm next," said Rachel West, head of subscriptions. "To get more subscriptions we need our pressmen to put the subscription cards in the newsstand papers like they're supposed to – for some reason a lot of them just don't do it. We need our telephone salespeople to call at least 15 people a day and to tailor their pitches to the people they're calling, maybe by mentioning a recent news story from their neighborhoods. And our delivery boys need to stop annoying the customers we already have by throwing their papers into puddles."

"Can you check to see whether those things are done?"

"We could check up on the pressmen with a scale. Each bundle of newspapers weighs half a pound more with the subscription cards. We monitor the salespeople the same way Marsha's people do, so they're no problem. The paper boys would be tougher, but I guess we could do spot checks by surveying subscribers."

"Very good," Haskins said. "J.J., could you create databases for all this information?"

John Jenkins, the company's information technology guru, nodded.

"Sure. I can set something up that would let the phone-call monitors and subscriber surveyors check off lists right in the database. Direct observations – like checking on the newsstand operators – could be entered on the spot via cell phone. And I'm sure I could come up with all kinds of charts and graphs that would show each employee's habits of either doing or not doing these things."

"Perfect. But before we get to that we'll need to warn people that we'll be watching."

Chapter 6

Appropriate Antecedents

Antecedents are all around us. Anything that instructs you to do or not do something – a stop sign at an intersection, instructions from your doctor, or a burning smell coming from your kitchen – is an antecedent.

Antecedents are events that trigger somebody to perform a behavior. In business, the communication of a goal is the most basic antecedent. The message can be communicated in person, over the phone, via electronic or paper mail, or through a Web site.

In a large company, the whole communication plan has to be pretty well thought through before a behavioral science program can be implemented. Sometimes it is just a matter of announcing a change, and people can run with it. Other times it requires tools and training – a much more complex process to go through to navigate the employees from where they are today to where you want them to be. In a large company there are many populations that collaborate to work toward a specific goal. The key is to ensure that every population is informed both about the overall goal and about its specific tasks in support of that goal.

Ideally the start of a behavioral-science based program would include a comprehensive communication program. If this is truly strategically imperative, it deserves more than just an email. There could be a meeting and possibly some training. Depending on what you want to achieve you might do some cheerleading to really get people excited, to make sure people appreciate that this isn't just a program, but that it's vital to the company's direction.

Varied approaches are important not only to communicate the importance of the program, but to make sure employees with different learning styles all understand. That's why you want to mix it up. Some employees just need to read to understand. Others are going to need more graphic orientation in an ad format, or the personal touch. What you will find is that the people who are on the front lines, since they are so busy and aren't reading a lot, will want more of the quick hit, like an ad type. If you want to emphasize it, just like you would for a consumer, you have to spell out the benefits to them. That would probably be better face-to-face.

If employees have access to an intranet, news about the new program can be communicated over several levels. When employees first come into the intranet site, they might see views from the president and CEO, and they could learn about general news of the company. Then they could click into an area focused on their division or department, where they would learn how their part of the company will work toward the executives' goals. Finally the employees could reach an individual page that would explain exactly what duties are expected of them and how they will be rewarded for performing them.

This material will probably remain on the Web site, which is always good because you want to have reminders. The program announcements could be connected directly to the individual behavior statistics and reward account. Employees can actually go look at the reward itself, or the nomination and report and see exactly what they did.

In addition to the standing policies, employees should receive reminders, perhaps in the form of email or some other newsletter. If there is a nomination program, requiring employee input, continuing communication will be especially important.

The more detailed the instruction or the work involved, the closer you will have to get to a personalized antecedent, meaning you are face-to-face or have an in-depth memo. When you are talking about generalized value statements or strategy, then you can go with a more general antecedent. At some point somebody is going to have sit down with each employee and translate that strategy for them. Once you have done that once or twice, posters and speeches from the president will now make sense to people. What most companies do is just throw posters out there.

A manufacturing company, for example, might have the slogan, "Dealers Come First." But ordinarily nobody would go to the assembly workers and tell them what that means to them. When a product goes out in bad condition, the dealer who sells it probably looses a customer for life. If nobody provides that extra bit of explanation, the slogan doesn't mean anything.

Even if assembly workers understand that they have to be careful with the product (a less than revolutionary idea, after all), very few companies use consequences to reinforce the correct behavior. The workers rarely get feedback when something goes wrong, or when it goes right. They are just plugging along, so the slogan has no effect where it should.

Sometimes the slogan might have a negative effect, because in reality, corporate communication often works like the children's game Telephone. The message is transformed completely by the time it reaches front-line employees. People will roll their eyes and say, "What's the flavor of the month this time?"

That's why combining general ideas with detailed instructions is so important. Employees should always have information about specific activities at their fingertips just by clicking through to the program detail.

If any part of the program changes, a little icon can appear on the side of the intranet interface, showing that there is something new. If the technology is not in place, other forms of notification must be used.

It's important to remember that new imperatives can take months to get disseminated within an organization. While the reinforcement of consequences should speed the process, frequent program changes could undermine the behavioral science. Eventually employees will ignore even the consequences, knowing that they are likely to change again soon.

Here are some suggestions for getting your employees fired up and keeping them fired up throughout the program.

1. Praise people publicly.
2. Issue a challenge.
3. Stage an old-fashioned pep rally complete with teams and cheerleaders.
4. Create and update a bulletin board so everyone knows where they stand in relationship to the goal.
5. Recognize progress toward tough goals and outline what still needs to be done.
6. Create motivational posters, memos, photos, etc. and place them around the office.
7. Have the president of the company (or a VIP) give a pep talk to your group.
8. Handwrite notes to your crew, send email periodically, leave inspiring voice mail messages, distribute frequent status reports – maintain an on-going dialogue with employees. It's a great motivator!
9. If possible, schedule a team dinner or outing.

10. Pass out team T-shirts.
11. Stuff an uplifting message in paycheck envelopes.
12. Schedule a special event like a picnic, seminar or field trip.
13. Cater an impromptu lunch.
14. Announce the status of the program over the PA system.
15. Speak with employees one-on-one about their contributions and brainstorm on ways to improve.
16. Acknowledge both effort and outcome.
17. Acknowledge mistakes and failures up front. By confronting these issues and talking about them, people learn and mistakes are reduced.
18. Adapt to change. If special or unusual circumstances arise, be flexible enough to go along with the changes.
19. Create a climate of consideration by saying "Thank you" and complimenting people sincerely.
20. Share the impact the results generate for the company.

You have to start the behavior with the antecedent, because you need a base line to work from. But that's not enough. You might say you want something done by Thursday. Your employees will get done only what you ask them to do. They won't necessarily do anything more. An increase or improvement in behavior is caused by a consequence, not an antecedent. That's why you need praise or recognition. Once you have a behavior to work with, you can start applying consequences.

The Springfield Gazette
Part 3

"I could have a memo ready by this afternoon."

Several people at the conference table jumped at the voice of the publisher's assistant, who had spoken for the first time this morning (or any other morning, as far as most of the executives could remember). But the young man's boss shook his head.

"No, we need more than that," Bill Haskins said. "We'll bring everyone we've mentioned together to discuss what we're doing. I'll have a separate meeting with the pressmen, since their shift doesn't overlap with anyone else's."

"But what are we doing?" asked Rachel West, who was in charge of the *Gazette*'s subscription department. "I understand that we'll be keeping track of whether they do the things we want them to, but you said we won't yell at them when they don't. So what will we do?"

"It's really a shame that this is such a novel idea, but we'll praise them when they *do* do what we want," Haskins said. "In fact, we'll do more than that; we'll give them points that they can use to buy things around town. The different activities each of you mentioned will be worth different amounts of points."

"Sounds complicated," said John Jenkins, the company's IT director. "How will people keep track of the system?"

"I'm glad you asked, because that will mostly be your job," the publisher replied. "The whole thing will be spelled out on the intranet, plus we'll make up some posters to hang in the pressroom, since the guys down there don't have computers in the building."

"I see – I could make up a separate page on the site for each job classification," Jenkins said.

"What about the people who run the newsstands?" asked Jim Watts, who was responsible for single-issue sales. "They're not on our intranet, and you probably can't even call them in for a meeting."

"No, Jim – you'll have to meet with them personally to start things off," Haskins said. "And as far as keeping them informed after that, there are only about 30 people in town who sell the paper, right? We'll start publishing a one-page newsletter for them and distributing it with the papers every week or so."

"So how are these points going to work?" asked West, who was still skeptical of the whole arrangement.

"That's the most important part of the whole plan," the publisher said. "Behavioral science tells us that consequences are what push people to continue – or to stop – behaving the way they do."

Chapter 7

Appropriate Consequences

We recommend using positive reinforcement as consequences. This allows employees to take control of their careers, because they know what their company values. They are now being given notice on a real time basis of how well they are doing. At the same time, they will notice the programs in which they're not being recognized, and – without needing to be criticized – they will try to improve in those areas to receive the positive consequences. Instead of working for six months and then sitting down in an evaluation to learn that he's been making the same mistake every day, the employee receives constant reinforcement.

In the sales world this approach is very common, in the form of commissions. Salespeople work hard because they know they will get a bonus after they get the sale. It's immediate: they have a positive consequence that is a certain reward.

The Problem with Money

But there's one element that many commission programs get wrong: they give salespeople extra money as a reward. Think about a child receiving an allowance: at some point she expects it. The money is no longer a reward for extra effort; it's how much she makes. How do most workers consider their Christmas bonus? Not as a bonus at all, but as a regular, expected part of their incomes.

Behavioral science says that you should use a 1:3 ratio – for every one time you use money, you should use praise or other rewards three times.

Of course the company will save money this way. But it's also more effective. Earning money doesn't make people feel special; it just makes them feel they are doing a job.

A lot of the difference between money and other rewards has to do with how each one is delivered and how much recognition employees get from their peers about it. Most analysts think recognition is much more important than the reward itself.

You could give someone a $2,000 bonus for doing something right, or during a staff meeting you could give him a letter telling him how important his behavior had been. The letter will encourage him to do it again.

On an informal basis, let's say one of the values of our company is to be open and honest. If 20 of us are sitting around talking about how to improve customer intimacy, and someone in the corner proposes an idea, and everyone laughs and makes fun of that person, he or she gets a consequence saying, "We don't really want you to propose an idea; we want you to follow our line of thinking." That is a consequence and would affect that person's behavior of coming up with an innovative idea next time. On the other hand, if the suggestion was immediately followed by eye contact or head nodding, praise or points, showing we actually do value openness and honesty, the person will feel encouraged. Whether or not we use the idea is not important. We just want employees to be free to come up with ideas – eventually some of them are bound to be useful.

There is nothing wrong with stepping out of your office and giving your employee a pat on the back, but if no one is around to see you do that it isn't as meaningful as it could be. Whereas using the internet, for example, you can give that person a pat on the back by putting it up on the Web where everybody can see the recognition. The employee is being recognized and knows that everybody else has seen it.

Recognition is a surefire way to make your employees feel appreciated and to reward them for their achievements. It inspires motivation, creates loyalty, and builds a positive, committed culture. Here are some ideas for ways to recognize your employees:

1. A personal note of acknowledgement
2. A small book of inspiring quotations
3. A surprise lunch
4. A personalized wall clock
5. Time off
6. A desktop game
7. Theatre tickets
8. A pat on the back
9. A trip
10. Hold a summer picnic
11. A pin denoting the achievement
12. A promotion
13. Pro sports game tickets
14. Gourmet food
15. A plant
16. A plaque decorated with an appropriate success philosophy
17. Limo service for a week
18. A magazine subscription
19. A personalized dictionary
20. Call a meeting to announce goal achievements

The subject of "Trophy Value" in incentive programs (as derived from the teachings of Richard Douglass) is really an issue of the difference between compensation and incentives, and how to use each in proper balance to achieve maximum results from your target audience.

It has been proven time and again that no incentive program will be truly effective unless there first exists a sound, well-conceived compensation plan. In the case of direct employees this means a proper salary, commission/bonus plan, and benefits package that will attract and retain the caliber of people necessary to carry out the corporate mission and to drive the long-term objectives of the organization.

In the case of distribution channels, the "compensation" plan relates to the combination of pricing, terms, commissions, rebates, discounts, marketing programs, etc., that allows you to attract and retain the best possible channel partners to market your products and allows those partners to derive an acceptable income for themselves in the process.

With either audience, a sound compensation plan is critical to marketing success and is a necessary precursor to any incentive program. It should be changed or manipulated as infrequently as possible since any change in the compensation plan – good or bad – will initially be perceived as negative, and it is very difficult to withdraw an element of the compensation plan once it has been offered. Compensation is perceived by the recipient as an "entitlement."

Incentives, on the other hand, are marketing tools to drive short-term objectives – such as introducing new products, opening new accounts, selling low-volume/high-profit products, or reinforcing new training activities. It is critical that these things be accomplished without making wholesale changes to the compensation plan because the objectives change so frequently. One of the big advantages of incentives is that they can be offered and withdrawn at will, without negatively impacting relationships with the audience. Incentives do not become an "entitlement."

So, why not cash incentives? If polled, most people will say that cash is the best motivator for them personally. After all, money has universal appeal. We all want it, and we can never seem to get enough. The recent advent of universal, or "unfiltered," debit and credit card incentive products has simply created another form of monetary awards. Participants simply use them to pay for the same things that they would otherwise pay for in cash. In essence, they are nothing but "plastic cash."

If money were the ideal motivator, however, commissioned salespeople would operate at peak efficiency at all times. What actually happens is just the opposite. The salesperson becomes "income adjusted," often resulting in one of two very undesirable results for an incentive program:

1. Participants earn the same amount of money for selling fewer products and services, or
2. Participants earn more money for selling the same amount of products or services

Either of these two scenarios can be disastrous in an incentive program. Yet both research and experience clearly indicate that non-cash incentives, in the form of merchandise and/or travel awards, are more successful than money as an incentive award. Why? The reasons are both psychological and symbolic. Non-cash awards *satisfy "wants" rather than "needs"* – Cash or cash equivalents, such a unfiltered debit cards, can be spent on everyday "needs" such as groceries, medical bills, or gasoline. But non-cash awards are used for "wants" such as a new jet ski, a new stereo or TV, or a trip to Hawaii. Satisfying a participant's "wants" is the role of incentives; satisfying "needs" is the responsibility of compensation.

eliminate guilt – Try justifying the purchase of a new set of graphite-shaft golf clubs to your spouse or family members when you are two months overdue on your rent. But if your incentive earnings can't be used to pay the rent, you're forced to spend them on your dreams and desires. Too bad! Since there is no choice, there is no guilt!

are demonstrable – Our culture does not permit us to boast about our income, our net worth, or the amount of our last bank deposit. Nor do we find much satisfaction in bragging about paying off an overdue bill. But boy, do we ever take pleasure in showing off our new car, or talking about our recent trip to Monte Carlo. Non-cash awards are tangible symbols of our success and provide an acceptable and important means for us to satisfy our emotional needs for peer recognition.

have memory value – That ring on your finger...do you remember when you got it? Who gave it to you? How you felt when you received it? Probably so. But who remembers (or wants to remember) where the last paycheck went? Non-cash awards provide a continuous, long-lasting reminder of one's success – and the efforts that went into achieving it – along with a fond remembrance of the person or company who gave it to them.

and are difficult to compete against – Cash awards can be easily countered (or bettered) by competitors, almost instantly. Non-cash awards, on the other hand, promote goal-setting and create "mind share" with your participants. When was the last time you didn't think about frequent flyer miles when you booked an airline ticket?!

The same intranet site can deliver the communication around the antecedents, can be used to make observations of behavior, and can govern the consequence system appropriately. It can actually be the delivery mechanism in points or dollars, or just be the reporting mechanism for anything intangible.

It's important for these recognitions to be purely positive. A lot of leaders serve the "innuendo sandwich" – they walk in and say, "You are special, but there are concerns about the way you have handled something, but overall you're a really nice person." They didn't say what the concerns or the issues were. They gave you some innuendo that something was wrong, but then they covered themselves by saying how nice you are. They've already done the damage by giving the criticism, but it's only an innuendo, so they can say they just complimented you. That's really poor leadership. People use it in companies to build political strength. It's unfair, wrong, and in the business community where you are trying to lead people, it can cause a company to become a gossip chain. It can be the death of somebody in the company who is really a valuable person.

When you give somebody a compliment and give him or her praise, recognition, or reinforcement, anytime you are giving something positive you should never mix it with something negative. If you have something negative to go to, wait for another time to do it. You can't do the two of them together. They dilute each other. You aren't going to get the behavior you want when you mix positive with negative. Nine times out of ten, the bad news will travel to seven people, compared with one who will pass along the good news.

Flexibility

If you're using material rewards in addition to praise, the key is that you keep consequences flexible. Depending on where employees are in their lives, they may truly want simply money, or they might need more time off, or they may need some other reward.

What turned me on yesterday might turn me off today and might turn you off tomorrow. As long as the company has a menu of rewards it can offer, you can let the employees tell you what it is that is going to motivate them. It doesn't even have to be one thing at a time.

The simplest way to be flexible is to use a point system that allows employees to "buy" different items with their points. But you don't ever want to give the impression that as opposed to trying to increase productivity you are trying to sell merchandise. You don't mark up the merchandise or keep a warehouse full of inflated value merchandise you are trying top push through to employees.

This is a system that allows the rapport between managers and workers to be open, honest, and dynamic so that if you are starting to go off track you can have an immediate adjustment and get back on track. When you know what constitutes success, you will do what you need to do because you will inherently want to win. When you get positive consequences, you want more of them. There are numerous examples demonstrating that humans always go after the pleasure principle. We want to be loved, accepted, recognized, and included. If we are getting feedback that we are doing the right thing, we kick into gear and do more of it because we want to be successful and to be proud. We will actually outperform our own expectations because we are getting that feedback that we are on the right track. We want positive consequences, even if they're not tangible.

Timing

Timing is a critical factor in any rewards system. If you don't get recognized until a month after you have done something, you have probably forgotten about it. The recognition doesn't have any meaning. If the praise or reward doesn't come on time, it can actually become a demotivator. If you want to change and then sustain behavior, you need to reinforce success directly.

You should even recognize employees for the same behavior repeatedly. Imagine that I praise you for something once. Then a few weeks later I see you doing the same behavior again and I come up and tell you that you are doing a great job, and I post on the bulletin board what a great job you are doing. Now you are getting some esteem out of it, and you are starting to like this because you are getting recognized. You know what I am measuring because I have told you. You know how to look at your accomplishments. We all want a measurement. The guy in shipping who used to ship 50 boxes now ships 20 because no one ever told him that was what they appreciated. The number one reason people leave a job is that they don't feel appreciated.

Too much praise will not do anywhere near the damage that no praise will do. The damage control is far worse when you are not doing it. In good leadership you have to have integrity and people following you. Managers often know that someone is doing a good job and end up taking them for granted and the behavior becomes extinct.

At the same time, being sincere about the praise is important. Good managers know the balance. They know when to go do it. There isn't a day that goes by when you shouldn't be praising someone, but you don't just pick out people at random and tell them they are doing a good job. At some point they are doing their job, and you recognize what they are doing. Praise has to be meaningful, and that's why you set up an approval system in a nomination-based program. Otherwise everyone will recognize everyone for everything. The managers can pick and choose how often they want to come in and look at the data, or they can identify threshold criteria. You don't want frivolous recognition; you want things tied to an objective that have a reinforcing effect on the employees.

People need to be acknowledged for their achievements and feel that they have an impact on the company. Here are just a sampling of ideas for reasons to recognize employees:

1. A creative idea
2. Consistent quality work
3. Continuous improvement
4. An extra-mile effort
5. Meeting the goal
6. Surpassing the goal
7. A winning attitude
8. Support
9. Loyalty
10. Punctuality
11. Cost-conscious behavior
12. Being part of the team
13. Strong leadership
14. Being fast and efficient
15. Being a tactful manager
16. Managing time wisely
17. Motivating others
18. Blazing new trails
19. Never quitting
20. Keeping well-read and informed

One way to limit the possibility of overkill is to use intermittent reward systems. You don't want rewards to spiral out of control, because you want room to continue the program. That's how gambling works. You keep playing this thing and once in a while you win – sometimes you win big. People really react to behavior reinforcement, and intermittent consequences in a lot of cases work better than continuous ones. Employees don't always get rewarded every time they do something good, it's only when they get caught and managers feel like doing it. But they have to do the right thing all the time because they never know when they are going to get caught and when managers might feel like doing distributing consequences.

You also might identify 10 behaviors but choose to award points for only six of them. You are letting employees know there are 10 things that are important, but right now you are focusing only on these six. Sometime in the future you might shift the groupings around.

The key to this whole thing is to take advantage of the latent capacity you already have. People really do want to work for the company, but they need a reason why, and they want to be recognized. If you are not going to recognize people and make their job situation any better, then you'd better pay them and let them figure out how to make themselves feel better. If management doesn't take control early with the number one tool that it has, appreciation, then labor will begin to take control. In the absence of any other incentives, people want more money and fewer work hours. One way or the other, the people are going to get something out of the situation.

Another form of encouragement is ranking people based on their performance. You might just show the top 10 because you don't want to embarrass those below. The crux of the decision is that you want to make public only positive things. You wouldn't want to put a trend report out in public, because that would show the things that you weren't doing so well. What you want to do is show the positives. If a piece of information is negative or neutral, leave it alone, until you can reinforce behaviors that will make it positive.

Letting other employees see each other's data is a privacy issue that each company must deal with on its own. Typically companies have handbooks that set the ground rules on how they are going to operate. Some companies will not let employees review their peers, just like most companies do not encourage sharing reviews with peers.

At least some pieces of data you will want to use for stimulation or peer pressure purposes. You might extract the best performer in a peer group category and post that person's score and what behaviors keep him or her at the top. You can do it that way, but it would probably be considered crude to post everybody's score, because it would be a demotivator and embarrassing for some of the bottom performers.

While all of this recognition can take place online, via an intranet or even mass email, we encourage offline recognition as well. You can use the computer to print out a certificate, but then you should take it to the person. Give both electronic recognition and personal recognition.

An electronic system could send an automatic card based on any particular behavior, but it's better for a supervisor to type in a message that is personalized. If employees know that they are getting a thank-you cards that were automatically generated, they aren't going to be excited. If they get a message and know that their supervisor was aware of them and involved, they are certain that that is good. A personalized message is successful reinforcement and is perceived as genuinely occurring.

Points

A point-system reward might work like this: If an employee is observed to be wearing a hard hat in a safety or construction zone, that observation is entered into the system and the employee is awarded so many points. Another example might be that a call center representative opens a call correctly, transitions to up-sell, and closes the call correctly, and the combination of those three result in the awarding of some number of points. In either case the result is communicated – through an email, perhaps – to let the worker know he or she has received an observation and the points along with it. Upon access of an account, the employees can see exactly how the points were earned.

The company can set up different ways for employees to spend points. One option is a virtual mall. They click on "shop," and up pops a substantial inventory of different vendors. Employees might have access to an internet portal, through which the points would be converted to dollars so employees could shop at any site on the Web. That can be more confusing to employees, however, particularly the ones who are not internet savvy.

Choice is good, but too much choice is bad. Generally a specific list that covers the gamut of retail industries works best.

A point can be worth any small value, perhaps from a penny to a dollar. As soon as employees click on shop, at the spot on the screen where they usually see points they now see dollars.

Another option would be to let people turn their points into cash that they would receive with their paychecks. We don't recommend that, because study after study has shown that recognition via dollars doesn't have the same trophy value. If people use their points to buy something, they associate that thing with the points they get from the company. If they take the money and throw it into their bank accounts, they are not sure if this money associated with a particular behavior paid for their electric bills or their medical bills. You do the same thing with gifts. If someone gives you a gift for your birthday, you tend to associate that gift with him or her. If someone gives you $20, and it goes in your pocket, you'll never know what you spent it on.

How do employees access these accounts? If the employees work with computers, supervisors don't want them looking at the points and spending them went they should be working. So the system might be accessible only from off-site, or only at certain hours. When there isn't technology available, the company can set up three to five workstations in a central area where people on break or at lunch can sit down, log in to the site, and have access. (Just establishing such an area creates another vehicle for all kinds of communication. Instead of using costly paper, now the company can broadcast information via this device.) The technology might also work over the telephone.

If you want the behavioral change very quickly then you need to make all these things available to employees when they have free time to get access to it. If you want the immediacy that will help speed up behavior change, it's better to create systems that are always active and catch employees on the fly while they are doing their jobs.

All of these activities have the added benefit of standardizing how reinforcement is done. In a large organization, that can be a real problem. You have some managers that are very good at managing people, recognizing them, and developing them, but some managers who just aren't. They might be more prone to micromanagement and are all over people, or maybe they just don't recognize them at the right times. If they program is electronic, the monitoring system itself can prompt managers to recognize and reward. Whether employees work for good managers or bad managers, or work in the local or foreign office, technology allows all the people to be treated equally and to have a standardized format for when they are evaluated and recognized for doing something well.

Though in general you should use only positive consequences, the system can also help managers who have trouble with reprimanding employees. Negative consequences can be sent simply in the data reports – feedback without points. Or you could subtract points. That is a way of saying you recognized what the person did, but it wasn't what you wanted. There is a system and infrastructure for sending the feedback. Instead of having to do the awkward and uncomfortable face-to-face critique, you are giving constructive feedback that comes immediately.

Instead of the manager's being the bad guy, the system shows the performance that the employee needed to reach and shows that he or she did not reach it. The manager is just the referee; the employee is responsible for his or her behavior. The system is much more fluid, objective, and effective when people can see their feedback on a real-time basis and you are not surprising them at the end of the year or quarter.

You can also simply ignore behavior you don't want, while you comment on and reward all other behavior. An employee's activities are all going to focus on where she is being rewarded.

All of these decisions about distributing rewards (or the lack of rewards) must depend on the individual employees. Some people will be more receptive than others to different consequences, and to these programs in general.

There are now many Web sites that try to determine what your interests are; the next time you visit the Web site it displays a banner ad targeted toward your interests. There are even some computer programs that try to figure out what you would want as a lottery prize. Managers should do the same thing. Some people respond to a new golf club or some other piece of merchandise. But an investment banker who makes $800,000 a year, for example, will not likely be interested in that at all. You inspire somebody like that with recognition and reinforcement. That is more important to those people. They already have won the toys game – they have them all. What they haven't won is recognition.

My philosophy is choice, choice, and choice. Your company may have a pre-established relationship with some merchants because of an existing incentive program. But up to a pretty high threshold, the more choices the better.

That's why points rather than specific rewards are so useful. A lot of times today, someone does something once and gets a gift certificate for a video rental or a restaurant. One reward for one-time activity. What we are trying to do is reward consistently over time so that people can accumulate points that they can spend however they like, or save. Instead of getting a small certificate, they can choose a $300 banquet at the French café downtown or an extra week of vacation. Choices are important. Instead of you as the manager trying to figure out what each employee will be motivated by, points give employees the ability to do that for themselves. They can choose between buying lots of smaller items or saving up for a large one. Managers might even be able to pass their points down to others as special bonuses to create new incentives.

In some situations some employees might be receptive to rewards within the work environment, which would be even cheaper for the company than points. In our company we have someone who is very new to marketing. She comes out of education administration and went back for her MBA. What is it that this person values? We know that what she values is learning as much as she can about marketing, so we reward her with more responsibility to create her own campaign with the company. We work with her to make sure she uses it properly.

You have to sit down with people – and a lot of companies don't – and try and understand their goals as individuals, and what are some of the things they like to do outside in the world. Those things are going to help you find the reinforcement mechanisms that will trigger them to want to perform. It will also help you find those intrinsic motivators that will cause them to perform. What really fires this guy up about the job that I can key off of and make work in other areas of the job?

Employees can also create their own performance objectives. There might be three or four goals that are company-driven, and one or two that are personally-driven. The latter might be in promotion or career growth, for example.

As Donna Deeprose wrote in *How To Recognize and Reward Employees* (New York: AMACOM, 1994), letting employees set their own goals is one way to establish intrinsic rewards at work.

Most of us can think of a time where we quit something or didn't follow through with a plan. Maybe it was an exercise program that didn't last more than three weeks. Or when you decided the diet you were on just didn't compare to that bowl of chocolate ice cream and bag of chips calling out your name. At work, have you ever felt like doing anything but the job you're supposed to be doing, so you just slacked off for the day?

The reason these attempts didn't last or the job didn't get done is that the motivation was not intrinsic. "Intrinsic" means innate or within. So intrinsic motivation is when your drive to succeed comes from within yourself. This type of motivation is especially relevant at work. When employees have intrinsic motivation, they are motivated by things like purpose, passion, and mission. Intrinsic rewards, Deeprose wrote, are "the good feelings people get from the work itself, feelings like enjoyment from the very act of performing the tasks involved, excitement about confronting and overcoming challenges, satisfaction in helping others or accomplishing something worthwhile, and pride in doing a job well."

The opposite of intrinsic motivation is extrinsic motivation. Extrinsic motivation comes from external motivators, like money, recognition, and rewards. Extrinsic rewards are effective, and they can be a nice way to show your appreciation to employees, but they will not provide the same lasting benefits that intrinsic "hot buttons" will.

Finding extrinsic rewards for your employees is easy. You can give out bonuses, gift certificates, meaningful gifts, or you might have an awards dinner to recognize outstanding achievements. But what about intrinsic rewards? After all, those come from within one's self, so how can a manager possibly give an employee an intrinsic reward or find that "hot button?" There are ways to promote intrinsic motivation in your employees, and although they may not be as straightforward or obvious as extrinsic rewards, they are even more powerful and meaningful.

One way managers can foster intrinsic rewards in their companies is to create the kind of culture in which workers will experience intrinsic motivation. This is an environment in which

- work is more fun,
- employees know the work they do is meaningful and worthwhile,
- problems are viewed as challenges, not as restraints,
- it's OK for employees to try new ways of doing tasks and to do new tasks that interest them, and
- employees know when they've done a good job.

The second way supervisors can promote intrinsic motivation is through empowerment. When employees are given more autonomy, they have increased satisfaction in their work because they have the power to pursue their ideas, use their best skills, and make important contributions to their company. This situation also increases your power as a manager, because you have a more efficient, productive, and innovative work unit. You can expand the power of your employees, by

- giving them the authority to set goals, make decisions, and solve problems,
- helping them to obtain necessary resources,
- facilitating their access to people who can give them the help and cooperation they need to accomplish their work (e.g. yourself, upper management, employees from other departments), or
- providing information. This item is especially important in organizations in a state of continuous change, because employees may feel powerless when they don't know what is going on. By relentlessly pursuing information about your company's mission, plans, financial status, and

progress toward meeting its goals, you can empower both yourself and your employees.

The third way to unleash intrinsic rewards in employees is through job enrichment. Job enrichment is increasing the scope of a job to provide workers with more challenges and more opportunities to expand their skills. It is not simply adding more meaningless or routine tasks to the employee's already existing duties. You can enrich an employee's job by giving them

- an opportunity to handle a project from the beginning to the end,
- a chance to develop new skills and demonstrate new competencies, or
- rotation to a project with high visibility in the organization.

When the effects of extrinsic rewards have worn off, intrinsic motivation will continue to drive a person to put forth his or her best effort. When people have intrinsic motivation, they will continue to strive to do their best regardless of whether an extrinsic reward is coming or not, because motivation resides in the employees themselves. Extrinsic motivators may attract people to your company, but it is intrinsic motivators that make them stay with you.

If a person's personal goals are truly personal, though, like getting into the workforce to find a spouse, that's inappropriate behavior. This system is not going to support that, but on the contrary it will suggest that that person needs to be elsewhere or needs a change of behavior. If an employee's personal goals aren't compatible with the company's goals, behavioral management will help highlight that immediately.

Did it Work?

One of the inherent problems of recognition is that you never know if it really makes a difference. The theory is that with recognition, especially with well-executed recognition programs, work improves; but because recognition is an after-the-fact display of appreciation for a job well done, it's difficult to prove.

For example, Jane has always performed her job reasonably well. Recently, however, she delivered a significant project two days before the deadline, so you thank her and take her to lunch to express your appreciation. In the days that follow, you notice that her performance has improved all around. She is more efficient, happier, and it seems as if she is putting out better work. Is it just a coincidence? Maybe Jane has been reading a motivational self-help book because she wants to improve herself, or maybe all along she's been a better employee than you thought. You just don't know.

Or, how about Robert. He's been the sales leader at your company for nine months. Because of his initiative and the business he generates, he receives more positive reinforcement than anyone else in the group. And every month he continues to perform exceptionally well. Coincidence? Is the recognition contributing to the consistent results, or is it something else? You just don't know.

Making a concrete determination of an employee's return on investment (ROI) is a near impossible task. To be able to identify the exact combination of factors that lead to an individual's success, or failure, is a science that no one has yet perfected. Part of the problem is that most of the factors affecting an employee's performance are not quantitative. For instance, how does one measure the effect of a kind word of appreciation or encouragement, or an exciting new personal relationship, or a dying parent, or even a headache? All of these factors may contribute to performance and the ensuing results, so how does one determine whether recognition makes any difference at all?

One of the best ways to judge the power of a recognition program is to determine the potential impact it can have on various areas of the employee's internal and external environment, and to actually measure the results. It's this value of impact (VOI) that is going to tell you whether or not your program makes any difference.

Culture

Potential impact: People who are recognized for their efforts have better attitudes toward their work. And when recognition goes on throughout an organization, the company becomes a better place to work.

Measurement: Distribute an employee assessment survey prior to and during a recognition program. See if employees' attitudes toward work, management and the organization change. Continue to review employee satisfaction at periodic intervals to assess the impact value of the program on an ongoing basis.

Customer Satisfaction

Potential impact: If the employee is happy, the customer will be happy. It may not always hold true, but how likely is it that an unhappy, unappreciated employee will serve customers well?

Measurement: Conducting formal surveys or asking for informal customer feedback may be the best way to get at the heart of this impact point. For instance, if customer comments become more positive after a recognition program is initiated, you can be pretty confident that the program is making an impact.

Attendance

Potential impact: For the most part, employees who come to work every day – on time! – are satisfied employees. This, of course, doesn't always hold true, but more than likely the ones who are often sick or late are not especially thrilled with the prospect of getting back to their jobs.

Measurement: This one is a no-brainer. Keep close tabs on absences and tardiness. And see if your recognition program has an impact on attendance.

Retention

Potential impact: Again, there are exceptions to the rule, but usually satisfied, happy employees are loyal employees. Companies with high turnover rates often have problems with morale.

Measurement: The value of impact of a recognition program can be evaluated by keeping track of turnover rates, and seeing if a year before the program the rates were any different from those a year into the program.

Productivity

Potential impact: Employees who feel their work is valued are much more likely to share ideas and work harder for the company.

Measurement: A subjective evaluation is not going to give you a valid assessment. Monitor specific performance metrics that the recognition is designed to reinforce, and then compare the metrics to productivity data collected before the recognition program. The impact value will speak for itself.

Determining the VOI will allow you to gauge the success of and cost-justify recognition programs. Given the potential impact that recognition can have in a company, understanding the VOI of a program can go a long way toward telling you whether recognition is "working." No one can account for all the factors that affect an employee's performance, but knowing – with confidence – one factor that can help boost it is half the battle.

Success!

A reward program should not stop dead as soon as the goal has been reached. In order to make the program meaningful and improve future incentive programs, it's important to communicate the results, analyze the results, and celebrate the success.

When communicating the results of the program, there are some rules that apply:

- Inform the participants of the results as soon as possible after the program ends.
- Highlight the strengths of the program, what worked well, and where the improvements or increases were made.
- Underscore the areas that can be improved further.

By keeping the participants informed and then following up in a timely manner with the results of the program, management will have set the stage for this final discussion.

As soon as the results have been tabulated, record observations about what worked and what aspects need improvement. There is no better time than immediately after a program ends to record observations and recommendations, while everything is fresh in your mind.

Analysis should be done in two distinct parts:

1. Analysis of what happened: Record what happened and why. What was the morale of the participants? What was some of the early feedback from the participants? What problems or obstacles did you encounter? Was there some particular part of the program that went extremely well?
2. Recommendations for the future: Take a few moments while everything is clear to make several recommendations for the next program. Perhaps outline a kickoff event you would like to try, different types of awards, different methods of measuring participant activity, or anything else you

feel would be appropriate information for the next program.

Here are some critical points in evaluating any incentive program:

- Name of program with a brief description
- Morale of participants
- Feedback from participants
- Feedback from managers/administrators
- Problems encountered
- Recognized strengths of the program
- Recommendations

After the results are in and announced, award distribution should soon follow. The sooner the award distribution is after the program, the more motivated the participants will be in future programs. When the award is immediate, it is more closely linked to the program and overall goal in the minds of the participants.

If the award is customized (e.g. needs engraving, screening, or etching), place the order as soon as the recipients are known. You may want to consider giving a companion gift or even a handwritten note immediately to capture and commemorate the accomplishment.

Presentation of the awards should be a planned event. Although it may not have been known exactly who was going to win, after the winners are announced, there is still opportunity to personalize the award presentation. Some people love a good show and are comfortable in the spotlight. Public recognition is well-suited to this type of individual. Presenting the award(s) at a party, dinner, meeting or convention with a great deal of fanfare would be appropriate for people who enjoy being publicly recognized for their efforts.

There are some individuals, however, who are extremely uncomfortable with any public attention. They much prefer to have their efforts recognized privately with their supervisors or bosses.

Presenting the award(s) face-to-face while verbally highlighting the employees' accomplishments would be appropriate for people who prefer being recognized privately for their efforts.

Following the three "post-program" steps of communication, analysis, and celebration can significantly improve the success of your rewards program and the success of future rewards programs in your company.

Celebrate Good Times

Not sure how to orchestrate that awards ceremony? Music, lights, cameras – it's a lost art, putting together a first class production, but it doesn't have to cost a lot. You can put one together for a lot less than you think. There are five basic steps:

1. Get the names of and some information about all of the people being recognized: what they achieved, their titles, and some past achievements. Write a three- to five-sentence paragraph in a PowerPoint slide presentation. Scan in their pictures so that on each slide is a person's picture along with his or her bio. If you don't have a laptop, rent one with Power Point on it, and pick up a projection system too.

2. Find a place to do the presentation that offers space, no distractions (such as phones ringing or

renovation in progress) and a respectable climate. A properly decorated space in the office could suffice but it's recommended you go to a local hotel and rent a seminar room. Decorate the area with a stage of some sort, and a podium, and a center aisle so people can easily walk to the stage. A tabletop podium can be purchase for around $100 and can be reused. Decorations, including a projection screen, can be had for less than $200. Don't forget music. Use something upbeat. You will want walk-in music as everyone gathers to take their seats. Play music with a strong beat and have it make some noise. A hotel can hook a player into the house system to get the effect you're after. If you're holding the event at the office get a stereo player, and remember, upbeat music creates excitement and gets the feet tapping. Set up the projector in a rear-screen format if you can. This way no one sees the projector because it's behind the screen. The person running the slide show can also run the music. Make sure you coordinate when to have the music on and off and practice working with the person running the slides. Have an opening slide for the event with some sort of title.

3. In preparation for the big event, send out an agenda with a list of the awards that will be given out. Make sure the people receiving awards will be there. Don't forget to hire a photographer. You can usually find professional-quality photographers at a reduced rate by going to high school or college newspapers. Have the photographer take crowd shots and casual shots as well as stage shots.

4. On the big day go through your setup, slides and any rehearsals an hour before the event. Five minutes before the event, begin playing the music, loud! Don't let people into the room until you see a crowd start to develop. A crowd generates excitement and the feeling that people are going somewhere special. Open the doors and get people to fill in the seats up front. The presenter should come up after everyone is seated. He or she should say a few words and then begin the presentation. As a name is called, the person's slide with picture and bio should come on the screen, and you could also play some music that fits the award (e.g., "Taking Care of Business" or "We are the Champions"). Don't play the same song over and over. Mix it up. Make sure the photographer gets a good picture.

5. Afterward, create a flyer or newsletter with the photos of the people on stage as well as photos of the crowd and any interesting shots. Make sure you put captions in place and title the flyer or newsletter. Give one to everyone who attended as a keepsake, and probably several to each of the people being recognized.

Just a little planning and a few added details like music, a professional photographer and a slide show can turn a so-so recognition event into the Academy Awards for your people. This little extra effort will make those being rewarded feel even more special and drive other employees through the next program.

The Springfield Gazette
Part 4

"Let's start with the ad reps," said Bill Haskins, the *Gazette*'s publisher. He turned to his director of advertising sales. "Marsha, you came up with five behaviors that you'd like to encourage. One involved the reps' going to the paste-up room every day to check on the ads, and the other four were things they're supposed to say during their phone calls."

"That's right," Marsha Jones replied. "But how many points should each one be worth?"

"Let's keep it simple to start – one point each," Haskins said. "You'll collect the sign-in sheet from the paste-up room each morning and enter the points into J.J.'s database. That way everyone should earn at least one point a day, so everyone will stay interested. The other behaviors will be spot-checked only periodically – and without warning, of course – but each call that gets monitored will be a chance for a couple of points. A call to check on an existing advertiser is worth one point automatically, plus one more if the rep makes a pitch for larger ads than the advertiser is already buying. Along the same lines, a call to a company that advertises with our competitors is one point right off the bat, and if they actually make a sale and recommend that the company designs its own ads, there's another point."

"Maybe we could do special campaigns, too," Marsha said. She lowered her voice to sound like an announcer's. "'This week is Customer Service Week, and courtesy calls to existing advertisers will be worth triple their usual value!'"

"Now you're getting the hang of it," the publisher said with a nod. "Let's move on to the newsstand operators."

Jim Watts, who oversaw newsstand sales, frowned.

"Do you really think the operators will be interested in these points?" he asked.

"They will once they see the list of high scorers in that newsletter," Haskins said. "They'll all be trying to beat each other. But they've only got three behaviors to work with, so maybe we should make one of them worth two points. Which one is most important?"

"Asking people who are buying other things if they'd like a paper too, definitely," Watts said. "They'll need a real incentive to talk to someone for a change. Those other things – giving us the best display spot and hanging up a full front page – shouldn't be too difficult."

"Good. Rachel, you're next. You had one behavior each for the pressmen, the subscription salespeople, and the paper boys."

Rachel West nodded.

"The pressmen and the salespeople are easy," she said, "one point for putting the cards into the papers and one point for making 15 phone calls properly in a day. But what about the paper boys? I said I wanted them to stop throwing the paper in puddles, but giving them negative points doesn't make much sense."

"No, it doesn't," Haskins said, "and we want to keep things positive anyway. What if we gave them points for perfect, welcome-mat deliveries? You could pick a couple of routes a day, secretly, and call a couple of subscribers at random and ask where they had found their papers that morning."

West agreed to make the calls, and the rest of the meeting went by quickly. Haskins explained that each point would be worth 10 cents. Employees – and the newsstand operators – would receive a list of stores where they could redeem their points: all they had to do was give the company their receipts and they would get reimbursed. They would also be allowed to buy extra vacation days.

The *Gazette* implemented the system soon after. At first, not many employees were enthusiastic – the points didn't seem to be worth enough money to get their attention. Haskins didn't want to increase their value, though, because of the attendant increase in cost to the company. Instead he instructed each of the department heads to adopt newsletters similar to those that went to the newsstand operators. Many employees, the salespeople in particular, soon dedicated much more energy to the appointed tasks – not for the money the points represented but for the competition. To inspire the last stragglers, and to make sure the competition stayed healthy rather than cutthroat, Haskins next ordered department-wide parties to congratulate employees for reaching various point milestones. At the parties staffers received certificates praising them for reaching 100 or 200 or 300 points.

With these adjustments, the program sparked exactly the progress the executives set out to achieve at that first meeting. In celebration Haskins gave everyone 500 bonus points – and then he set slightly higher targets for the next six months.

Chapter 8

Behavioral Science at Home

You have probably realized that you can apply the principles to behavioral science to your life at home – especially if you have kids.

One of our employees, for example, has a son who has behavioral problems. He is very impulse oriented, like a young child. He will pick up sticks and throw them at people. Our employee uses the behavioral science method to change his son's behavior. His son gets rewarded when he is polite to teachers or acts politely in the home. He is constantly rewarded for the positive things he does in a positive way. If he does something negatively, he does get negative reinforcement to try and extinguish the behavior.

If you see your child behaving in a way you would like to change, keep a record of the incidents. Just like our system keeps a record of evaluations over time to show a trend, if you have a spreadsheet, you could put dates across the top column, and then have the behaviors you are looking for as the rows. You can plug in "Yes" or "No" when the child acts well or poorly. You reward good behavior. Over time you can look at the spreadsheet and it will show a success rate over the number of days that have been filled in. You can see if the child is getting better or worse.

The reason that is good is that to be able to have something physically to look at or to show the child will reinforce the behavior. Otherwise people look at things as a snapshot. Parents generally can tell you how much their child is doing something, but they have no concrete data to support what they are saying; it is anecdotal. This record system would give you a tool to use. If you have to go see a doctor about it, then you have data to show.

Many parents keep these sorts of charts of medical issues when their children are young. But at some point we stop doing that with our children and just fly by the seat of our pants. If we were a little systematic we would see some trends developing.

Behaviors you could reward positively might include earning good grades or cleaning up rooms. In the past, parents gave up in a lot of areas because experts say kids need their space. Let's say it's just cleaning the bedroom or helping around the house. What you need to do is develop a system so you can see when it's done and when it isn't. Some parents have used casino-style chips. Those act as points. Every time the children are good, they praise them and give them chips. The chip can be used to purchase TV time, or to be driven to get ice cream.

Don't mix it up with allowance, because a lot of experts feel that children should expect to do certain things around the house not for money. So if you give them an allowance, don't use the money as a reason for them to work around the house. Sooner or later they will say they don't need the money – once they get a part-time job of their own, for example – so they don't need to help out around the house. With a work-based allowance you are training them not to do anything except for money. What you want to do is train them to be a part of the family and to accept responsibility. You can praise them and use a points system. That separates it, and is praise oriented.

The chips are used for certain privileges, and that's different form using money. A personal choice reward has more meaning to make them try to do things the right way. A lot of times, parents don't give a good choice of rewards to kids. If the choice is something they don't want, they won't care and won't change their behavior. If a parent wants the children to come home and do homework right after school, then every third day they can be praised or rewarded. The value you have is on learning and not going out and playing. That's a good way. It's just like a company. My strategy as a parent is for my kids to grow up and be smart. I do want them to be well-rounded and go out and play, but I don't want them to spend more time playing than studying. If my number one value is to make sure they learn, then I should praise them when they exhibit learning behavior. That could be choosing to watch the Discovery Channel rather than cartoons. If you reward those types of things, they will get the idea that this is a good thing to do.

Maybe you want them to try new things. Good nutrition is a big issue for many families. Most people try to sneak it into their meals. You reward them and show them that it is important to at least try their vegetables. They may spit it out. For example, I hated squash and my dad used to put heaping amounts of it on my plate. Everything surrounding squash was a punishment. I wouldn't get desert until I ate squash. He not only created a negative atmosphere, but he also lost the debate eventually. What he should have said was just try a little bit. If he did that, then he could praise me for at least trying. That teaches trying. You aren't going to like everything. That's really what he should be rewarding – the effort. The end result may not be what you want, but if you reward the effort of trying, then that person will continue to try other things. That's really what is important. This is a very common issue for parents.

Food, homework, helping out around the house are all common issues that can be attacked with this system. Praise or a point system really works well with all of them. As adults, we are so tight for time, so we need everybody to pitch in. If you make a big deal out of efforts your children put in, you'll find that kids are always looking for ways to help. They won't just sit and wait to be asked to do things. They will ask if you need help setting the table, etc. That's hopefully what you raise your kids to be like.

There will come a time when they are teenagers when you need to be reminded of the good things that they do. It's very common today because of the time pressures we are all under that we don't spend enough time finding out who did what and thanking them.

You see cases on the news of kids who have gone wild. The big thing that comes out is that those kids think their parents don't care about them or pay enough attention to them. That tells you right away that they are not reinforcing good behavior and showing those children that they appreciate and love them for being there. That's a big issue. It's never too late to create a system. Maybe if the child is older, you can be more subtle about it and not keep a chart, but you can make notes somewhere so you can be reminded and praise them accordingly. Most parents don't do that. They constantly reprimand their teenagers, and only use antecedents. It's better to use positive reinforcement. There will come a time when you have to tell them not to do something, but while you are doing that make sure they know that they have also done some things right.

It's the behavior itself and the immediate consequence to that behavior that shapes the behavior. When the child touches the stove and it is hot, that consequence of getting burned is what stops the behavior from being repeated. That's in the negative sense. The positive sense is in the same way. Who hasn't gone to a Little League game or musical and watched their child perform - they always look to you for acceptance and approval. They behave accordingly. That's behavioral science right at its core. We all do it constantly every day.

Chapter 9
Case Study I

The Business Case

A phone company needed to significantly increase employee productivity and sales without compromising customer service in a large metropolitan area call center.

Background

In the fall of 1999 the phone company's Customer Center initiated a systematic, online performance improvement program developed, implemented and managed by CultureWorx. Their goal was to achieve a significant increase in sales by selling in a manner both pleasant for customers and productive for the phone company, without sacrificing service quality.

Using Internet-based performance management software, which records behaviors and instantly delivers rewards as points into employees' electronic virtual accounts, or eV accounts ™ , teleservice representative (TSR) coaches remotely observed representatives. In addition, TSRs had the ability to freely access their personal performance information or point balances in their eV accounts and redeem points directly online for products at brand-name retailers.

CultureWorx online performance improvement program has been in place at the center for more than one year. Tangible and anecdotal results show that it has consistently maintained a positive impact on employee behaviors and, as a result, on sales. In addition, this reinforcement-based program has transformed the culture at the call center from one of management-by-the-numbers and crisis-of the-moment to an atmosphere of high energy that is performance driven with engaged employees.

Tangible Results

The call center has consistently ranked first out of 15 like centers in sales and support, a significant improvement from averaging ninth place one year ago. The center has also been named the winner of a regional performance contest and has broken the company record in its number of calls per 100 converted to sales (C-Order Rate). In addition, the company has seen a significant increase of 40 percent in overall customer satisfaction scores. In light of these benchmarks, the center has been granted an expansion, adding 100 new seats, which will make it the company's largest call center. In addition, the center has been designated as a leadership incubator for cultivating leadership roles for employees, coaches and management staff.

Continuous Improvement

Because the program involves random, remote observations of TRS' performance in real time, employees received immediate, relevant feedback. TSRs had the ability to view their own areas of strengths and weakness and use specific information to improve their call flow behaviors right away. The system also enabled the coaches to spot performance issues and address them with additional coaching or training as required after the initial surge in productivity of more than 20 percent. In response to this method of instantaneous feedback, individuals and teams showed an average 2 percent increase in monthly performance improvement across the board, boosting their yearly performance levels to 24 percent.

Anecdotal Results

The company also experienced a change in employee attitude regarding the performance evaluation process. In the past employees and managers considered evaluations a negative aspect of their jobs. Managers didn't know how to provide constructive feedback, and employees felt emphasis was placed on their shortcomings.

After implementation of the system, both groups began viewing performance evaluations in a positive light. They realized it created a positive performance evaluation process and contributed to an environment of high-achievement orientation. TSRs receiving positive reinforcement and rewards have been more likely to request remote observations and feedback. Team pride and friendly team competition have also compelled employees to continuously enhance their performance.

As a result, awards are recognized as status symbols among the employees, fully integrating the program's reward system into the center's culture. The evident success of this program has led to behavior-based performance evaluations and awards for the entire center.

Program Satisfaction

The implementation of the program involved the installation of systems and technology new to the managers and coaches. To their credit, these leaders not only overcame their resistance to these new tools but embraced them in their workflow management, even autonomously recording observations at home on the Internet.

The TSRs' eagerness to collect and save points has been measurable. For example, redemption rates routinely peaked during the holidays, special computer kiosks that allowed employee access to their accounts were filled during work breaks and TSRs frequently requested awards be shipped to the center so they could show coworkers what they earned. In one team of five women, each redeemed points for the same designer purse, each in a different color. These illustrations show how the point system has become a positive aspect of the company culture. In regard to point redemption, online reward redemption has been consistently favored nine to one over gift checks. This 15-month review of the online performance management program at the Customer Center demonstrates the program's success has been significant and consistent over time. Employees are dynamically involved in refining their performance, overall customer satisfaction has substantially improved and sales continue to increase.

These charts summarize the key points of this case study:

The Solution Framework

The system is comprised of three key components:
- Consulting: involves reviewing processes, pinpointing specific behaviors that contribute to corporate goals, and training managers.
- Technology: provides a way to automate and analyze performance feedback.

- Rewards: offer employees positive reinforcement and come in a variety of forms.

The Return On Investment (ROI)

As a result of the program, the company exceeded its quarterly goals and increased employee performance in several areas:
- Year-to-date CQC scores - 7%
- Use of a transition statement - 7%
- Tailoring suggestions - 20%
- C-Order Rate - 20%
- Customer satisfaction - 40%
- Reduced turnover - 10%

Bottom Line Impact

Increase in center revenue from $45 million in 1999 to $50 million in 2000 from recognition to tangible items.

Award Mix

Reinforcement	Recognition	Rewards
Feedback	Spotlight on success using electronic message display boards	Tangible points to b redeemed online at leading, brand-name retailers
Positive performance observation	Recognition billboard	Discretionary spending account for employee perks

Praise: one-on-one and in group setting	Recognition lunches	Promotions and pay increases linked to performance
	Spontaneous celebrations	Trips

Cultural Transformation

- Performance expectations are clearly communicated
- Desired behaviors are positively reinforced
- Initiated performance feedback loop
- Achieved high-profile success within company
- Leadership incubator
- Enhanced employee satisfaction and pride in the team's accomplishments

Critical Success Factors

Internal Support	**External Support**
Committed leadership team	Technology infrastructure
Management accountability	Behavioral pinpointing correlated with results
Training and coaching	Regular recap/review process

Chapter 10
Case Study II

Name: Quill Corporation

Location: Lincolnshire, Illinois

Type of   Business-to-business office supplies direct marketer & call
Company: center

Number of 1,200
Employees:

In an environment where salespeople may never see many of their customers, companies must make the most of every opportunity to gain sales. In a brick-and-mortar environment, that's done with point of purchase displays in the checkout line. On the phone it's done by offering sale items to every customer. Quill Corporation believes those incremental sales are so important that they figure prominently in employee performance evaluations.

"We utilize the CultureWorx program for our incremental sales program to award points to associates who offer our sale items to phone customers, regardless of whether or not the customer actually makes a purchase," says sales manager Kim Kelly. "Points also are awarded to associates for actual incremental sales. Every associate who makes a sale is rewarded by earning points."

Actually tracking these points and using them as key factors in performance reviews, Kelly says, has boosted incremental sales. "More associates are winning points than ever before, and our incremental sales have increased during the past six months."

HR consultants have known for years that behavior-oriented appraisal and tracking systems foster improvements. Results tracked by such systems are quantifiable and objective, and let employees know exactly how they're doing in a way that provides more information than the too-often-heard comment, "You're doing OK."

The CultureWorx system strengthens relationships between managers and employees not only by helping to provide objective feedback, but also by doing it in real time, continuously. As a result, managers can reinforce positive behaviors as they occur. This encourages employees to form effective habits and stops bad habits before they can form.

Kelly's experience only emphasizes that idea. She says, "The CultureWorx program allows me to communicate and administer our incremental sales reward program in an efficient, effective manner, while at the same time, allowing our people to be proactive" about tracking their own progress.

Traditionally, managers focus upon corporate directives and policies to improve employee performance. This takes up about 80 percent of a manager's time but delivers only 20 percent effectiveness, according to Craig Muller, chairman of CultureWorx. Kelly adds that there's "a huge benefit in allowing our associates to take ownership of their incentives. We feel that this truly motivates them." One of the reasons is that consequences are aligned with behaviors and with corporate goals, so employees see the relationship between their performance and those objectives.

Coaching is an integral part of Quill's program. It's also an area that needs improvement, according to the SHRM "2000 Performance Management Survey." Only half of the managers surveyed are trained to provide feedback. "Performance software is not a substitute for face-to-face coaching sessions," Kelly says, "particularly in a high-pressure, high-stress area like a call center, employees need sincere praise, positive feedback, and development opportunities that are discussed with them one-on-one."

For managers, such real-time, continuous-feedback systems can help them provide specific performance information before ineffective behaviors become bad habits. They also allow them to make strategic adjustments within their departments to better align their work to corporate goals. In the case of incentive rewards, CultureWorx keeps the corporate goals to the fore, helping employees avoid tailoring their goals to particular incentives.

Administrative ease is another benefit, Kelly says. Quill has eight distribution centers in the United States and a warehouse in the United Kingdom.

Because the program is Web-based, it can be accessed easily from any location, providing complete information each time. "The program provides an accurate account of all the happenings of the program in one centralized format. As the administrator, I have the choice in how much actual hands-on work I need to take part in."

Workforce, **April 2001, pp. 78-79**

Chapter 11
Case Study III

Chemicals Manufacturing and Marketing

This Fortune 50 operating company's CEO chartered a blue-ribbon task force to identify cost-cutting opportunities. Improvements from the company's quality and reengineering initiatives had reached a plateau. However, it was clear that there were still many opportunities for achieving better results. The task force's investigation revealed that the barrier to reducing costs was the company's culture, which was top-down, authoritative, and did not systematically reinforce employees' taking responsibility and initiative for improvements but instead reinforced buck passing, hiding both opportunities and problems, and avoiding responsibility.

Solution Implemented:

The project recognized that the company's culture was the consistent patterns of behavior that were systematically reinforced. It set about planning and carrying out an initiative to develop the behaviors identified as crucial to the success of the company. The initiative included coaching in productive management and the use of positive reinforcement. Each executive's and manager's objectives were cascaded to reports. Accurate measurement of performance on objectives was established and tracked through results scorecards. Leadership scorecards were developed to ensure that all executives and managers lead the right way. Managers throughout the company were trained in the use of positive reinforcement and the scorecards. Teams were set up to identify and improve upon process problems through focused projects. Specific

150

best practices were developed to address such common problems as planning and sorting out roles and responsibilities.

Specific activities included:

1. Redesigning three major performance systems (performance appraisal, job selection, and career development) to support a culture that reinforced cost management.
2. Providing education and coaching for all leaders – from the CEO to first-level supervisors.
3. Tracking progress and results by designing and implementing a balanced scorecard system with monthly tracking, cascaded throughout the organization.
4. Training people to apply the tools and methods themselves so that the organization could continue applying the tools and methods without external support.
5. Design and execution of a company-wide Vision Performance Conference to involve the top 250 leaders in the new vision and strategic objectives.

Results of Intervention:

The CEO publicly recognized the initiative as the finest, smoothest, and most well-received performance improvement initiative in the company's history.

The following company-wide improvements were achieved:

- 30 percent average improvement on balanced scorecard indicators within 6 months.
- $45 million annual savings resulting from improved plant reliability, including a 75 percent decrease in plant shutdowns.
- Improved from worst to first among all corporate operating companies in the employee commitment index, including eliminating all 9 "vulnerabilities" identified in the survey.

Targeted programs within specific sites and departments tallied additional results:

- 550 percent improvement in the number of savings incidents, as a result of improved purchasing effectiveness.
- Improved the percent of on-time shipments from 15 percent to 98 percent.
- 27 percent increase in compliance with use of personal protection equipment.
- Reduced plant operating expense, reducing spending to 12 percent below budget.

Chapter 12
Case Study IV

Food Distribution Services

This food distribution company began to experience pressure on profit margins as competition in its industry increased. To protect the interests of shareholders, senior management decided to reduce the cost per case of food handled by improving employee productivity. Unfortunately, the initial efforts got results – but in the wrong direction, as both costs and customer complaints increased. Knowing that its desired outcome was valid and possible, the management team identified that work processes, measures, and behaviors needed to be aligned.

Solution Implemented:

Distribution centers were shown how to develop integrated cost, quality, and customer service metrics and to change behavior systematically among front-office staff, warehouse technicians, and drivers. The center's compensation system was modified and aligned with work processes and the value delivered to the customer.

Results of Intervention:

- The number of "perfect" deliveries increased, as did customer satisfaction.
- Operating costs in the centers that participated in the alignment dropped by 15 percent to 20 percent.
- Significantly improved collaboration among the front office, warehouse, and delivery reduced the number of re-orders and re-deliveries.

Chapter 13
Case Study V

Marketing & Sales

The Mexican unit of a major oil company brought in a new general manager to improve operations. Since the economic collapse in 1994 and 1995, the organization had had difficulty meeting its targets and had recently implemented a 20 percent downsizing. In addition, the parent organization had just announced its intent to merge with another company. The leaders of the Mexican unit sought help to keep people's "heads in the game" during the merger and simultaneously to improve the business performance of the organization. Specific improvements were targeted in controlling expenses and increasing sales in "high-value" customer segments of the market.

Solution Implemented:

Executive coaching helped the executive team identify and accept accountability for both results and leadership behaviors. Leadership development and coaching for the top 20 leaders of the organization was implemented. The coaching focused on creating high performance leadership behaviors to keep key people focused during potential merger distractions and to drive operating performance improvements. Leaders learned to set clear expectations, to hold people accountable for their commitments, and to provide positive and constructive feedback frequently. In particular, the leaders built an effective accountability management system around balanced scorecards, which were put into place immediately prior to the development and coaching.

Results of Intervention:

- Reduced annual expenses and achieved a $2 million cost savings in the first year after the intervention.
- Achieved record sales and profitability in the history of the business unit.
- One region turned around its profitability in one year from 0 profit to $2.5 million in profit.
- The fuels side of the business, which measures its costs in cents per gallon, took enough cost out of the ongoing business to reduce costs from 5.4 cents per gallon to 3.8 cents per gallon, resulting in savings of $1.2 million annually.
- Significantly improved collaboration of sales, operations, and marketing team members.
- The process was successfully transferred so that the general manager continued to facilitate the use of Coaching Action Plans for improving performance.

Chapter 14
Case Study VI

Nitrogen Products

This major chemical manufacturing company chose an "injury-free work environment" as a strategic objective. Employees had not exceeded 30 injury-free days and needed to make significant improvements in their performance.

Solution Implemented:

A leadership team of more than 100 executives, managers, supervisors, and safety personnel were trained to identify and pinpoint key critical safe behaviors (CSBs) of individuals and teams. Leadership team members developed Coaching Action Plans to help others increase their CSBs in order to positively impact the targeted business measures. Critical unsafe behaviors were also identified for reduction. Performance Coaching involved helping the 100 members of the leadership team implement their Coaching Action Plans. This led to positive changes in the day-to-day performance and behavior of approximately 1,100 employees. Executive Coaching helped the leadership team members improve their own coaching and influence skills and employ reinforcement-oriented coaching techniques rather than the punitive techniques that had characterized some past approaches to improving safety.

Results of Intervention:

- Achieved a record six months injury free during formal tracking and reported that the record was sustained several months beyond tracking.
- OSHA recordable incidents declined from the three-year average of 5.73 to 3.52 during the seven-month consulting engagement.
- Wearing of safety glasses improved from 70 percent to 99 percent.
- Wearing of aprons in the magnesium plant improved from 90 percent to 100 percent.
- Successful housekeeping inspections improved from 70 percent to 99 percent.
- Over 50 "Critical Safe Behavior" Coaching Action Plans were implemented successfully.

Chapter 15

Worksheets

Worksheet 1
Setting Goals

The first step is a brainstorming exercise: Think of as many goals as you can that could help your company (or division or team) improve its performance. You might want to use the big three categories to jump-start your thinking.

Increased Sales	Decreased Costs	Better Customer Service

From your lists, pick 10 goals that are most critical. Rank them, noting the numbers next to each item.

164

Worksheet 2
Setting Goals, Continued

Next you need to narrow that list of 10 down to three or four that you will actually use. To do this you must look ahead a bit. Using the chart below, rate how well the descriptions in the first column match each of the goals you have identified. Use 10 to signify a very accurate description and 1 to signify a completely inappropriate description.

Descriptions\Goals from Worksheet 1	1	2	3	4	5	6	7	8	9	10
Improved performance will improve the bottom line.										
Improved performance depends on discrete, observable employee behaviors.										
Improved performance is clearly measurable.										
Improved performance is achievable.										
Performance can,										

theoretically, be improved indefinitely.													
Improved performance would not conflict with other critical goals.													
Total													
Average rating (total divided by 6)													

The average rating of each goal – the higher the better – will give you some sense of how valuable it is to you and of how easily it could be improved by applying behavioral science. Also consider how easy it will be for you to implement the system with the employees who would be involved: some companies might have an easier time with white-collar workers, while others might have an easier time with blue, for example.

Write your three or four selected goals below:

Goal 1:_____

Goal 2:_____

Goal 3:_____

Goal 4:_____

Worksheet 3
Pinpointing Key Behaviors

List the groups of employees that could play a part in achieving each goal.

Goal 1	Goal 2	Goal 3	Goal 4

List the specific behaviors employees must perform to achieve each goal, numbering the behaviors associated with each goal from 1 to 10.

Goal 1	Goal 2	Goal 3	Goal 4

Worksheet 4
Pinpointing Key Behaviors, Continued

Next you need to narrow the list of behaviors associated with each goal to a manageable number – no more than five for any single group of employees. Using the chart below, rate how well the descriptions in the first column match each of the behaviors you have identified. Use 10 to signify a very accurate description and 1 to signify a completely inappropriate description.

Goal 1

Descriptions\Behaviors	1	2	3	4	5	6	7	8	9	10
Improved performance would lead to achievement of the stated goal.										
Improved performance is achievable.										
Performance can, theoretically, be improved indefinitely.										
Improved performance is easily measurable.										
Improved performance would not conflict with other critical behaviors.										
Total										
Average rating (total divided by 5)										

Goal 2

Descriptions\Behaviors	1	2	3	4	5	6	7	8	9	10
Improved performance would lead to achievement of the stated goal.										
Improved performance is achievable.										
Performance can, theoretically, be improved indefinitely.										
Improved performance is easily measurable.										
Improved performance would not conflict with other critical behaviors.										
Total										
Average rating (total divided by 5)										

Goal 3

Descriptions\Behaviors	1	2	3	4	5	6	7	8	9	10
Improved performance would lead to achievement of the stated goal.										
Improved performance is achievable.										
Performance can, theoretically, be improved indefinitely.										
Improved performance is easily measurable.										
Improved performance would not conflict with other critical behaviors.										
Total										
Average rating (total divided by 5)										

Goal 4

Descriptions\Behaviors	1	2	3	4	5	6	7	8	9	10
Improved performance would lead to achievement of the stated goal.										
Improved performance is achievable.										
Performance can, theoretically, be improved indefinitely.										
Improved performance is easily measurable.										
Improved performance would not conflict with other critical behaviors.										
Total										
Average rating (total divided by 5)										

The average rating of each goal – the higher the better – will give you some sense of how valuable it is to you and of how easily it could be improved by applying behavioral science. List your selected behaviors on the next two pages, noting whether each one will be observed by management, by peer employees, or by employees themselves and whether each one will be measured quantitatively (done or not done) or qualitatively (done well or not well, on a scale).

Worksheet 5
Pinpointing Key Behaviors, Continued

Goal 1

Behavior	Observed by	Quant. or Qual.

Goal 2

Behavior	Observed by	Quant. or Qual.

Goal 3

Behavior	Observed by	Quant. or Qual.

Goal 4

Behavior	Observed by	Quant. or Qual.

Worksheet 5
Appropriate Consequences

Finally, you must formulate a system of consequences –
and stick with it. On this page and the next, list the
consequence with which employees will be rewarded for
carrying out the behaviors you have specified.

Goal 1

Behavior	Consequence

Goal 2

Behavior	Consequence

Goal 3

Behavior	Consequence

Goal 4

Behavior	Consequence

Chapter 16

The Future of Employee Relationship Management

Vision

These behavioral systems will be to behavior management what Microsoft is to personal computers: the operating system underlying and energizing human effort throughout an organization and acting as the common platform for infusing successful behaviors into all processes.

Mission

Businesses will develop systems that maximize the value of human capital by energizing employees and infusing successful behaviors into organizational processes, which subsequently increases productivity and profits.

Values

Businesses will use these types of behavior operating systems to instill and reinforce their values throughout their organizations so that their unique personalities and differentiation will ring through all the noise and clutter in their marketplaces.

Why It's Different

A behavioral operating system takes proven behavior science principles and infuses them into a software technology, empowering companies to implement the successful techniques of managing behaviors and activities with consequences.

There are plenty of software technologies that collect and report on an abundance of information within your company, but none actually provide you with a tool to create change based on that information. Consequences act as a change agent, reinforcing the right activities and extinguishing negative behaviors or activities that don't help achieve your objectives. Behavior software not only collects the information but automates consequence-reinforcement so your employees become self-directed, understanding, in real time, what's expected, what they've done correctly and what activities are less desirable.

Chapter 17

Review I

Each day at work, your computer is monitoring your every move. When your activities contribute to the company's bottom line, you earn points that can be redeemed for a reward of your choice—and you get immediate kudos from your boss.

Sound enticing, or a bit Orwellian? It's the theory behind CultureWorx, a Web-based behavior management system that assesses employees and gives them incentives.

The software takes a page from well-established behavioral science: if you encourage preferred behavior rather than reprimand negative behavior, people will naturally continue acting in a way that rewards them.

"If you want to shape a behavior, you have to have consequences," says Bruce Moeller, president and CEO of the CultureWorx company. "The more immediate and certain those consequences are, the more it will shape a behavior, and it's the behavior of employees that creates a [corporate] culture."

Like Pavlov's dogs, people can be conditioned to expect a specific consequence to specific actions. If fulfilling a task in five minutes means a greater reward than doing it in 10 minutes, chances are they'll complete it in five minutes. This relationship is not lost on U.S. employers, who spend approximately $26.8 billion annually on incentives, according to *Incentive* magazine's 2001 survey.

Earning Points

With CultureWorx, the consequences associated with preferred behavior are points that can be redeemed for prizes of the employee's choice. (Employees are not docked for undesirable behavior.)

"A person may want to use the points for something tangible or intangible—recognition, extra time off, stock options, whatever it takes you to be motivated," says Moeller. CultureWorx does not depend on profit from point redemption, he adds.

CultureWorx connects with existing systems, like an automated call distribution system, to monitor associated activities. Each employee accesses their information via an individual Web page that shows their tasks, how well they fulfilled them and a tally of their points. When information on an individual's page changes, they're notified via email. When points are earned or a summary report added by a "mystery observer" or supervisor, the employee receives immediate feedback.

Working the Phones

Quill, a direct marketer of office supplies and products, has been using CultureWorx for the past 10 months. Quill currently has 1,200 employees and has gone through several employee reward and recognition programs, says Kim Kelly, marketing and recognition administrator for customer relations.

At Quill, CultureWorx can award points to employees who offer incremental sale items to phone customers, Kelly says, and the points don't depend on whether the customer actually makes a purchase. Results are tracked each week.

The program seems to pay off, Kelly says. "Incremental sales have increased over the last six months and we closed our 2000 fiscal year with almost a $2.5

million increase from the previous year. I believe a significant portion of this can be attributed to CultureWorx."

Employees at Quill balked at the idea at first, because it was Internet-based and very different from the traditional review process, Kelly said. In addition, employees might wonder about issues of privacy or feel uncomfortable about being monitored so closely and constantly.

The behavior CultureWorx tracks is no different than what a regular employer would track on paper, Moeller responds. Data is stored on servers maintained by MPX, an Internet hosting company that provides tight data security, he adds.

Technology Review, July 9, 2001, "Good Employee! Here's Your Reward," by Lisa Moskowitz

Chapter 18
Review II

CultureWorx' concept is innovative and unique and appears to be successful at aligning organizational strategy with employee performance. CultureWorx is designed primarily for mid-size to large organizations; most have some form of established and predefined core competencies or values that can be easily translated into measurable tasks.

However, the application is best suited for organizations where work processes are measurable and repeated. On the other hand, there must be enough differentiation within tasks and values for performance to be measured. In fact, it would be highly counterproductive to simply measure quantitative aspects to an individual's job. Therefore, the business and work structure must be able to support the CultureWorx concepts and goals; CultureWorx will not work well in all organizations.

Currently, the categories of industry that are currently using the system are within transportation, financial services, and call centers. In fact, call center-type work processes are ideal as they are continuously repeated and often highly monitored.

However, the concept behind CultureWorx can actually be used in your organization along different levels. For example, CultureWorx can be an indirect performance appraisal system. We've discussed the problems associated with annual or semi-annual performance evaluation; they are subjective, they don't properly reinforce behavior, there are misunderstandings, and little subsequent action is taken to improve or change behavior.

CultureWorx provides a unique alternative that isn't intrusive as semi-annual performance evaluations. Instead, behavior can be noted and recognized on a daily or weekly basis. Feedback is instantaneous and the application allows employees to monitor, judge, and reflect upon their past behavior. The feedback provided is positive and employees can indirectly see where their performance weaknesses are. Therefore, you can also see how CultureWorx can be used as an indirect performance evaluation tool as well as a strategic tool for rewards and recognition.

One unique aspect about CultureWorx associated with the aforementioned comments is its instantaneous feedback and reward structure. In a sense, the human critical element that employees take so personally during evaluations is removed but is still present as employees can observe their performance gaps over time. Instead, it is replaced with positive reinforcement and an observable rewards structure that employees can self-monitor over time. Organizations can develop and pre-determine their mission-critical values and behaviors, and align their workforce's activities and tasks with the values.

One of the goals of the Cultureworx application is to facilitate and promote consistent and timely communications across the entire organization. The home page of the application is designed to communicate announcements, goals, strategy, and organizational news. The concept of direct communication in combination with feedback loops and continuous positive reinforcement provides organizations with an effective means to interact, reward and direct their workforce.

There are a few fundamentals to successful positive reinforcement and proper rewards and recognition programs:

1. Identify the desired behaviours that should be rewarded.

189

2. Maintain an inventory of rewards that can be used as a positive reinforcement tool.

3. Recognize individual differences: We're all different, and a reward that would be of value to you, may not have as much value to another.

4. Ensure everyone in the organization knows exactly what must be done to receive a reward.

5. Administer the reward, immediately upon witnessing the desired behaviour or accomplishment.

Organizations forget about and under-utilize the power of positive reinforcement.

You can see that CultureWorx's application includes each of the fundamentals to a T. Although B. F. Skinner, the father of positive reinforcement theory, developed this theory in the 1940s, more than 60 years later, we're integrating the latest technology and his theory to reinforce positive employee behavior to create organizational success.

HR.com, "CultureWorx: Human Performance Management Software," by Katherine Lee

Appendix

Below you will find biographies of some of the key figures whose ideas underlie the application of behavioral science to business management, as well as more detailed discussions of their theories.

1. B.F. Skinner

Bio

Burrhus Frederic (B.F.) Skinner (1904-1990) majored in literature at Hamilton College in New York. After an unsuccessful attempt at becoming a writer, he went to Harvard to study psychology. Skinner found himself more and more a behaviorist. He worked in the lab of an experimental biologist, and developed behavior studies of rats. He designed boxes that would automatically reward behavior, such as depressing a lever, pushing a button, and so on. These devices became known as Skinner boxes.

In 1931 Skinner received his Ph.D., and in 1936 he took a position at the University of Minnesota where he wrote *The Behavior of Organisms* and began his novel *Walden Two*. He also began development of his controversial "baby box," a controlled-environment chamber for infants. Skinner often used pigeons as his experimental subjects, because they roosted outside his office window. With pigeons, he developed the ideas of "operant conditioning" and "shaping behavior." Skinner compared this type of learning to the way children learn to talk – they are rewarded for making a sound that is sort of like a word until in fact they can say the word. Skinner believed other complicated tasks could be broken down in this way and taught.

After nine years in Minnesota, and three years as head of the psychology department at the University of Indiana, Skinner became a professor at Harvard, where he remained for the rest of his life.

Theory of Operant Conditioning

B.F. Skinner's entire system is based on operant conditioning. Operant conditioning is when a behavior is followed by a consequence, and the nature of the consequence determines the likelihood that that behavior will recur in the future. An organism is constantly "operating" within its environment. During this "operating," the organism may encounter a reinforcing stimulus, or reinforcer. This stimulus increases the "operant," which is the behavior that occurred right before the reinforcer. The probability of that operant behavior happening in the future is increased.

	Increase Behavior	Decrease Behavior
Positive Stimulus	Positive Reinforcement (add stimulus)	Response Cost (remove stimulus)
Negative Stimulus	Negative Reinforcement (remove stimulus)	Punishment (add stimulus)

Types of Conditioning

Positive Reinforcement – Positive reinforcement is when a behavior occurs and a desirable consequence is given. Using positive reinforcement increases the likelihood of a behavior occurring in the future. For example, if a rat pushes a pedal and receives a food pellet, there is a greater probability that the rat will push the pedal in the future.

Extinction/Response Cost – When a behavior is no longer followed by the reinforcing stimulus, the result is a decreased probability that the behavior will occur in the future. This can eventually lead to extinction of the behavior, when it no longer occurs.

Punishment – The opposite of a reinforcing stimulus, an aversive stimulus is something that is unpleasant or painful. If a behavior is followed by an aversive stimulus, the result is a decreased probability that the behavior will occur in the future. This type of stimulus is used in the form of conditioning known as punishment. For example, if a rat performs a particular behavior and is shocked, there is less of a chance that the rat will perform that behavior again.

Negative Reinforcement – If an already aversive stimuli is removed after a particular behavior is performed, this is called negative reinforcement. Negative reinforcement increases the likelihood that a behavior will occur in the future.

Schedules of Reinforcement

Skinner also looked at what he called "schedules of reinforcement." He observed how different schedules of consequences affected the tendency of an organism to perform a behavior in the future. Following are the different schedules of reinforcement Skinner studied:

Continuous Reinforcement – Whenever a behavior is performed, a person/animal receives the reinforcing consequence.

Fixed Ratio Schedule – Every set number of times the behavior occurs the reinforcing consequence is given. The ratio may be three to one or 20 to one, but every three times (or however many is chosen) the behavior is performed the person or animal receives the consequence.

Fixed Interval Schedule – This is based on a time schedule. There is an amount of time allotted, say 30 seconds, and if the behavior is performed during those 30 seconds the reinforcer is given. If the behavior does not occur, there is no reinforcing consequence. But even if the behavior occurs numerous times within the 30-second period, the consequence is given only once. Skinner observed in the rats he studied that they tended to pace themselves. They would slow down the rate of their behavior right after the reinforcer and speed up when the time for it got close.

Variable Schedules – A variable ratio means that the number of times a behavior needs to occur before the reinforcer is given changes each time. First the behavior may need to occur four times before the consequence, then ten times, then one time, and so on. A variable interval means that the time period the behavior needs to occur in once to receive the reinforcer changes each time. First 15 seconds, then seven, and so on.

Skinner observed that the variable schedules kept the rats on their toes, because they could no longer pace themselves or establish a rhythm between the behavior and the reward. The variable schedules are also very resistant to extinction, because even if the re-inforcer hasn't been given for a while the mentality is that it could happen the very next time the behavior occurs.

Shaping

"Shaping" came from the question of how to deal with more complex behaviors. Skinner developed the idea of shaping, or "the method of successive approximations," to teach these behaviors. Shaping begins by reinforcing a behavior that is vaguely similar to the desired behavior. Once that behavior is established, when variations occur that are closer to the desired behavior those can be rewarded. This can be continued until the behavior you want is being performed. The idea of shaping can create a behavior that would not show up in ordinary life.

Behavior Modification

Behavior modification is a therapy technique based on Skinner's work. The technique involves extinguishing an undesirable behavior by removing the reinforcer for the undesired behavior, and replacing it with a desirable behavior using reinforcement. This can be used to help many problems including addictions, shyness, neuroses, and autism.

Source:
www.pbs.org

Books by Skinner:
About Behaviorism (1976)
The Behavior of Organisms (1991)
Science and Human Behavior (1970)
Walden Two (1976)

2. Edward Deming

Bio

W. Edward Deming (1900-1993) developed his "System of Profound Knowledge" as a comprehensive theory for management, providing the rationale by which every aspect of life may be improved. He also developed 14 points for transforming management. Deming's teachings of his management philosophy in Japan from 1950 on created a total transformation in Japanese business resulting in what is known today as the Japanese Industrial Miracle. In recognition of his achievements in providing the theory and methods to improve the quality and dependability of manufactured products, Deming was decorated by the Japanese Emperor with the Second Order Medal of the Sacred Treasure. In 1950 the annual Deming Prize(s) were established by the Union of Japanese Scientists and Engineers (JUSE).

For more than 40 years Deming served as a consultant in statistical studies with a worldwide practice. His clients included railways, telephone companies, carriers of motor freight, manufacturing companies, hospitals, legal firms, government agencies, and research organizations. Deming also published numerous articles and books and lectured at seminars and universities worldwide. He was on the faculty of the Stern School of Business at New York University for 46 years. He held a Ph.D. in mathematical physics from Yale University. He was elected to the National Academy of Engineering in 1983, inducted into the Science and Engineering Hall of Fame in 1986, and received the National Medal of Technology from President Reagan in 1986.

Theory

Deming provides an outside view on management called a System of Profound Knowledge, because he believes the prevailing, Western style of management is in need of a transformation. An organizational system cannot understand itself, which is why an outside view is required. The System of Profound Knowledge provides a map of theory to guide us in understanding the organizations in which we work.

The first step to begin the transformation is with an individual, and once the individual understands the system he or she can apply it to every kind of relationship. The individual will

- set an example,
- be a good listener, but will not compromise,
- continually teach other people, and
- help people pull away from their current practice and beliefs and move into the new philosophy without a feeling of guilt about the past.

The layout of the System of Profound Knowledge has four parts:

- Appreciation for a system
- Knowledge about variation
- Theory of knowledge
- Psychology

Deming developed 14 points to transform the present Western style of management to one of optimization. Deming's 14 points, excerpt from *Out of Crisis*, by Edward Deming, for management are as follows:

1. Establish constancy of purpose toward improvement of product and service, with the aim to become competitive and to stay in business, and to provide jobs.
2. Adopt the new philosophy. We are in a new economic age. Western management must awaken to the challenge, learn their responsibilities, and take on leadership for change.
3. Cease dependence on inspection to achieve quality. Eliminate the need for inspection on a mass basis by building quality into the product in the first place.
4. End the practice of awarding business on the basis of price tag. Instead, minimize total cost. Move toward a single supplier for any one item, on a long-term relationship of loyalty and trust.
5. Improve constantly and forever the system of production and service, to improve quality and productivity, and thus constantly decrease costs.
6. Institute training on the job.
7. Institute leadership. "The aim of supervision should help people and machines to do a better job. Supervision of management is in need of overhaul, as well as supervision of production workers.
8. Drive out fear, so that everyone may work effectively for the company.
9. Break down barriers between departments. People in research, design, sales, and production must work

as a team, to foresee problems of production and of use of the product or service.

10. Eliminate slogans, exhortations, and targets for the workforce asking for zero defects and new levels of productivity. Such exhortations only create adversarial relationships, as the bulk of the causes of low quality and low productivity belong to the system and thus lie beyond the power of the work force.

11.

    a. Eliminate work standards (quotas) on the factory floor. Substitute leadership.

    b. Eliminate management by objective. Eliminate management by numbers, numerical goals. Substitute leadership.

12.

    a. Remove barriers that rob the hourly worker of his right to pride of workmanship. The responsibility of supervisors must be changed from sheer numbers to quality.

    b. Remove barriers that rob people in management and in engineering of their right to pride of workmanship. This means abolishment of the annual merit rating and of management by objective.

13. Institute a vigorous program of education and self-improvement.

14. Put everybody in the company to work to accomplish the transformation. The transformation is everybody's job.

Fourteen points excerpted with permission from The MIT Press from Deming's *Out of the Crisis*.

Sources:

Deming, Edward. *The New Economics for Industry, Government, Education*, 2nd ed. Cambridge, MA. Massachusetts Institute of Technology, Center for Advanced Educational Services, 1994.
Deming, Edward. *Out of the Crisis*. Cambridge, MA. Massachusetts Institute of Technology, Center for Advanced Educational Services, 1986.
www.deming.org

Books by Deming:
The New Economics: For Industry, Government, Education (1997)
Out of the Crisis (2000)
Some Theory of Sampling (1990)

3. Frederick Herzberg

Bio

Frederick Herzberg (born in 1923) is considered the father of job enrichment, a pioneer in motivation theory, and one of the major management philosophers of our time. In 1946 he received his B.S. from City College of New York. He then went to the University of Pittsburgh and was awarded an M.S. in Clinical and Industrial Psychology, and soon after he earned his Ph.D. After being the research director for Psychological Services of Pittsburgh from 1951 to 1957, he became a professor of psychology at Case Western Reserve University in Cleveland. During this time he also served as director of the graduate program in industrial mental health. In 1972 Herzberg became a professor of management at the University of Utah. He spent the next 20 years consulting with government and industry leaders throughout the world. Herzberg is a believer in the Behavioral School of Management.

Theory: Motivation-Hygiene Model of Management

Herzberg studied a group of employees to find out what made them satisfied or dissatisfied about their jobs. He asked the subjects two sets of questions:

- Think of a time when you felt especially good about your job. Why did you feel that way?
- Think of a time when you felt especially bad about your job. Why did you feel that way?

Herzberg based his theory on a study of need satisfactions and on the reported motivational effects of these satisfactions. His study focused on 200 engineers and accountants. The subjects named different kinds of conditions as causes of each of the feelings. For example, if recognition led to a good feeling about the job, the lack of recognition was seldom indicated as a use of bad feelings.

Based on his study, Herzberg came to two conclusions:

1. Some conditions of a job operate primarily to dissatisfy employees when they (the conditions) are not present. However, the presence of these conditions does not build strong motivation. Herzberg called these hygiene factors, since they are necessary to maintain reasonable level of satisfaction. Some hygiene factors are:

- Company policy and administration
- Technical supervision
- Interpersonal relations with supervisor
- Interpersonal relations with peers
- Interpersonal relations with subordinates
- Salary
- Job security
- Personal life
- Work conditions
- Status

2. Some job conditions build high levels of motivation and job satisfaction. However, if these conditions are not present, they do not prove highly dissatisfying. Herzberg described six of these motivational factors, or satisfiers:

- Achievement
- Recognition
- Advancement
- The work itself
- The possibility of personal growth
- Responsibility

From the results of his study, Herzberg developed the motivation-hygiene model of management. The model states that employee motivation is achieved with challenging, enjoyable work where achievement, growth, responsibility, and advancement are encouraged and recognized. The environmental or hygiene factors, such as poor lighting, ventilation, poor working conditions, low salaries, and poor supervisory relations, serve as dissatisfiers.

Job Enrichment

Herzberg extended Maslow's ideas and made them more applicable to the work situation. He has drawn attention to the critical importance, in work motivation, of job-centered factors. His insight resulted in an increased interest in job enrichment, an effort to restructure jobs to increase worker satisfaction. If managers focus only on maintenance factors, motivation will not occur. The motivators must be built into the job to improve motivation.

Source:
Donnelly, James, James Gibson, and John Ivancevich. *Fundamentals of Management*, 10th ed. Boston, MA. McGraw-Hill, 1998.

Books by Herzberg:
Job Attitudes: Research and Opinion (1957)
The Motivation to Work (1959)
Work and the Nature of Man (1966)

4. Abraham Maslow

Bio

Abraham Harold Maslow (1908-1970) was an American psychologist and behavioral scientist. His "Hierarchy of Needs Theory" was first presented in 1943 in the U.S. Psychological Review and later developed in his book *Motivation and Personality*, first published in 1954. His concepts were originally offered as general explanations of human behavior but quickly became a significant contribution to workplace motivation theory.

Maslow was one of the first people to be associated with the humanistic, as opposed to a task-based, approach to management. As people have increasingly come to be appreciated as a key resource in successful companies, Maslow's model has remained a valuable management concept.

Theory: Maslow's Hierarchy of Needs

Maslow's theory of motivation stresses two fundamental premises:

1. "We are wanting animals whose needs depend on what we already have. Only needs not satisfied can influence behavior. In other words, a satisfied need is not a motivation.
2. "Our needs are arranged in a hierarchy of importance. Once one need is satisfied, another emerges and demands satisfaction.

Maslow identified five levels of needs, which he placed in a framework according to levels of importance. If all of a person's needs are unsatisfied at a particular time, satisfaction of the most predominant needs is the most pressing. Those that come first must be satisfied before a higher-level need comes into play.

Framework for hierarchy of needs

Physiological needs – This category consists of the human body's primary needs, such as food, water, air, and sex. Physiological needs dominate when they are unsatisfied, and no other needs serve as a basis for motivation. For example, if a person were lacking food, safety, love, and esteem, the hunger for food would be stronger than the other three needs.

Safety needs – When physiological needs are adequately met, the next higher level of needs assumes importance. Safety needs include the need for security, protection, and stability in the physical and interpersonal events of day-to-day life. This includes protection from physical harm, ill health, economic disaster, and the unexpected.

Social needs – These needs are related to the social nature of people and their need for companionship. The need for love, affection, and a sense of belonging in one's relationships with other people. Nonsatisfaction of this level of need may affect the mental health of the individual.

Esteem needs – The need for both awareness of importance to others (self-esteem) and actual esteem from others is included. A personal sense of competence and mastery is included in this need, and the need for esteem of others includes respect, prestige, and recognition. Esteem from others must also be felt as warranted and deserved. Satisfaction of these needs leads to a feeling of self-confidence and prestige.

Self-actualization needs – This is the highest need level: the need to fulfill one's self, to grow and use one's abilities to the fullest and most creative extent. The external aspects of self-actualization will vary as the role of the individual varies – a college professor versus a corporate manager versus a parent. The satisfaction of the self-actualization needs is possible only after all other needs are satisfied. Maslow also proposes that the satisfaction of the self-actualization needs tends to increase the strength of other needs. When people are able to achieve self-actualization, they tend to be motivated by increased opportunities to satisfy that need.

Characteristics of self-actualizers:

(Not all self-actualized people show all of these characteristics.)

- Perceive reality accurately. Not defensive in their perceptions of the world.
- Have an acceptance of themselves, others, and nature. Acceptance is not the same as happiness.
- Spontaneity, simplicity, and naturalness. Do not live programmed lives.
- Problem-centered. Possibly the most important characteristic. Have a sense of mission to which they dedicate their lives.

- Like privacy and detachment. Enjoy being alone; can reflect on events.
- Freshness of appreciation. Don't take life for granted.
- Mystic or peak experiences. A peak experience is a moment of intense ecstasy, similar to a religious or mystical experience, during which the self is transcended. People become so totally involved in what they are doing that they forget all sense of time and awareness of self.
- Social interest.
- Profound interpersonal relationships. Tend to attract admirers or disciples.
- Democratic character structure. Display little racial, religious, or social prejudice.
- Creative. Especially in managing their lives.
- Resistance to enculturation. Are autonomous, independent, and self-sufficient.

Becoming self-actualized does not happen overnight. Listed below are some behavioral exercises to try:
- Pay attention to the world around you.
- Make risky choices. Try to expand your world and learn from failures.
- Trust yourself more.
- When in doubt, tell the truth. This will simplify your life.
- Recognize the need for discipline. Get the requirements of life out of the way quickly.
- Cultivate peak experiences. The best way to do this is to pay attention to the world and your feelings.

- Give up your highly-valued pathologies. Get rid of psychological garbage.

Source:

Donnelly, James, James Gibson, and John Ivancevich. *Fundamentals of Management*, 10th ed. Boston, MA. McGraw-Hill, 1998.

Books by Maslow:
The Farther Reaches of Human Nature (1972)
The Maslow Business Reader (2000)
Maslow on Management (1998)
Motivation and Personality (1976)
Toward a Psychology of Being (1998)

5. Henry Mintzberg

Bio

Henry Mintzberg is the Cleghorn Professor of Management Studies at McGill University in Montreal, Canada, and a professor of organization at INSEAD in Fontainebleau, France. He is the director of the International Masters Program for Practicing Managers, a partnership of five business schools around the world.

Theory

Mintzberg grouped managerial activities and roles. The theory behind these groupings is that as senior managers play their roles, they will all come together as an integrated whole, reflecting the managers' competencies associated with the roles. They act as evaluation criteria for assessing the performance of a manager in his or her role. The activities and associated roles are as follows:

Managerial Activities	Associated Roles
Interpersonal relationships – arising from formal authority and status and supporting the information and decision activities	Figurehead Leader Liaison
Information processing	Monitor Disseminator Spokesman

Making significant decisions	Initiator/Improver/Changer Disturbance Handler Resource Allocator Negotiator

Explanation of Roles

Figurehead – Social, inspirational, legal, and ceremonial duties must be carried out. The manager is a symbol and must be on hand for people or agencies that will deal only with him or her because of status and authority.

Leader – The leadership role is at the heart of the manager-subordinate relationship. The manager

- defines the structures and environments within which subordinates work and are motivated,
- oversees and questions their activities to keep them alert,
- selects, encourages, promotes and disciplines, and
- tries to balance subordinate and organizational needs for efficient operations.

Liaison – The role of liaison refers to the manager's being an information and communication center. It is important to build up favors. Networking skills to shape and maintain internal and external contacts for information exchange are essential. These contacts give access to "databases" such as facts, requirements, and probabilities.

Monitor – A manager seeks and receives information from a variety of sources to evaluate the organization's performance, well-being, and situation. Monitoring of internal operations, external events, ideas, trends, analysis, and pressures is vital. Information to detect changes, problems, and opportunities and to construct decision-making scenarios. The monitor role is about building and using an intelligence system. The manager must install and maintain this information system by building contacts and training staff to deliver information.

Disseminator – In the role of disseminator, the manager brings external views into the organization and facilitates internal information flows among subordinates.

Spokesman – This is a role in the public relations capacity. The manager informs and lobbies others who are external to his or her organization. Key influencers and stakeholders are kept informed of performances, plans, and policies. The managers are considered expert in the field in which their organizations operate.

Initiator/Changer – The manager develops and initiates much of the controlled change within an organization. When gaps are identified, and improvement programs are defined, the manager initiates a series of decisions and activities to achieve the actual improvement. The manager can either delegate all design responsibility to select subordinates; empower subordinates with responsibility for the design of the improvement program but define parameters and give the go-ahead before implementing different aspects; or directly supervise the design of the program.

Disturbance Handler – The disturbance handler role involves taking charge when the organization unexpectedly hits "an iceberg" and when there is no clear programmed response. Disturbances can arise from staff, resources, threats, or mistakes made by others. The manager steps in to calm matters, evaluate, re-allocate, and provide support.

Resource Allocator – Manager oversee the allocation of resources. This role involves scheduling their own time, programming work, and authorizing actions. The manager sets organizational priorities and ensures that the basic work system is in place.

Negotiator – The managerial role of negotiator is taking charge of important negotiating activities with other organizations. The spokesman, figurehead, and resource allocator roles demand this.

Mintzberg developed conclusions based on these managerial roles. The roles point to the necessity of managers' being organizational generalists and specialists because
- of system imperfections and environmental pressures,
- their formal authority is needed for certain basic routines, and
- in all of this, managers are still fallible and human.

The roles offer an account of managerial tasks, and they explain managerial purposes in terms of
- designing and maintaining stable and reliable systems for efficient operations in a changing environment,

- ensuring that the organization satisfies those who own and control it, and
- maintaining information links between the organization and players in the environment.

Books by Mintzberg:

Mastering Strategy: Complete MBA Companion To Strategy (2000)

Mintzberg On Management: Inside Our Strange World of Organizations (1988)

The Rise and Fall of Strategic Planning: Reconceiving Roles for Planning, Plans, Planners (1993)

Strategy Safari: A Guided Tour Through the Wilds of Strategic Management (1998)

Structure In Fives: Designing Effective Organizations (1992)

Structuring of Organizations (1978)

6. Ivan Pavlov

Bio

Ivan Pavlov (1849-1936) was born in a small village in central Russia in 1849. His family hoped that he would become a priest, and he went to a theological seminary. After reading Charles Darwin, he found that he cared more for scientific pursuits and left the seminary for the University of St. Petersburg. There he studied chemistry and physiology, and he received his doctorate in 1879. He continued his studies and began doing his own research in topics that interested him most – digestion and blood circulation.

His work became well known, and he was appointed professor of physiology at the Imperial Medical Academy. Pavlov was looking at the digestive process in dogs, especially the interaction between salivation and the action of the stomach. He realized they were closely linked by reflexes in the autonomic nervous system. Pavlov wanted to see if external stimuli could affect this process, so he rang a bell when he gave the experimental dogs their food. After a while, the dogs – which before salivated only when they saw and ate their food – would begin to salivate when the bell rang, even if no food were present. Pavlov investigated this phenomenon and established the laws of classical conditioning. Classical learning was the first type of learning to be discovered and studied within the behaviorist tradition.

In 1904 Pavlov won the Nobel Prize in physiology/medicine for his research on digestion. He worked actively in the lab until his death at age 87.

Classical Conditioning

In classical conditioning, there must exist a stimulus that will automatically or reflexively elicit a specific response, such as blinking when air is blown in your eye. There are no new behaviors learned in classical conditioning; rather, an association is developed between two stimuli, one unconditioned and one neutral, so that a person or animal reacts to them both with the same involuntary response.

The specific model for classical conditioning is:

1. An unconditioned stimulus elicits an unconditioned response. A stimulus will naturally and automatically bring about a reflexive response. This stimulus is called unconditioned because there is no learning involved in connecting the stimulus and response. An example of an unconditioned stimulus would be holding food out in front of a dog, and the unconditioned response would be the dog's salivating.

2. A neutral (or orienting) stimulus does not elicit the response of interest. This stimulus is described as neutral because it does not elicit the unconditioned (reflexive) response. The neutral stimulus could be ringing a bell near the dog. The dog would show orientation but not the specific unconditioned response of salivation.

3. The neutral (orienting) stimulus is repeatedly paired with the unconditioned (natural) stimulus. During conditioning, the neutral stimulus will be presented and immediately followed by the unconditioned stimulus. Over time, the learner will develop an

association between these two stimuli. For example, the dog will make the connection between the ringing bell and the food's being presented to him.

4. The neutral stimulus is then transformed into a conditioned stimulus. Now when this new conditioned stimulus is presented by itself it elicits the conditioned response, which is the same as the unconditioned response. Although the two responses are the same, they are labeled differently because they are caused by different stimuli. Using the example, the ringing bell is now the conditioned stimulus, and the conditioned response is the dog's salivating.

Source:
www.pbs.org

Books by Pavlov:
Psychopathology and Psychiatry (1994)
Conditioned Reflexes: an Investigation of the Psychi (1978)

Bibliography

Blanchard, Kenneth and Spencer Johnson. *The One Minute Manager*, Berkley Books, 1982.

Braksick, Leslie Wilk. *Unlock Behavior, Unleash Profits: How Your Leadership Behavior Can Unlock Profitability in Your Organization*, McGraw Hill, 2000.

Buckingham, Marcus and Curt Coffman. *First, Break All the Rules: What the World's Greatest Managers Do Differently*, Simon and Schuster, 1999.

CIBC World Markets, Inc. *Employee Relationship Management*, Equity Research, Feb. 21, 2001.

Daniels, Aubrey C. *Bringing Out the Best in People: How to Apply the Astonishing Power of Positive Reinforcement*, McGraw Hill, 2000.

Daniels, Aubrey C. *Performance Management: Improving Quality Productivity Through Positive Reinforcement*, 3d Ed., Performance Management Publications, 1989.

Lehman, J. and T. Berg. *Managing Human Capital in the New-Economy Enterprise*, Strategic Analysis Report, The GartnerGroup, Jan. 29, 2001.

Lehman, J. *Human Resources: Outside the Comfort Zone*, Research Note, The GartnerGroup, Sept. 17, 1998.

Lehman, J., *Human Capital Management: Out of the Hands of HR*, Research Note, The GartnerGroup. 22 Feb. 2000.

About the Authors

Bruce Moeller

As CultureWorx' President and CEO, Moeller's goal is to establish standard operating systems for human behavior such that businesses can use rewards, recognition, incentives, and dynamic pay on an immediate and certain basis to shape corporate behavior. This tool allows predictable and sustainable results with human capital so that corporations can lead their organizations to results with leading rather than lagging indicators. Moeller has over 25 years of sales, marketing, operations and general management experience with major corporations such as Bell & Howell, ITT, GD Searle, and Mutoh America. At CultureWorx his role is to revolutionize how corporations lead their human capital with this unique tool for ensuring desired results from human beings operating as an Application Service Provider. Moeller has a Bachelors of Science in Business Administration from Pacific Western University and has always been an innovative growth oriented leader who has focused upon leadership as his key area of interest and expertise.

Craig Muller

Founder and Chairman Craig Muller leads the team at CultureWorx, an Internet-based business-to-business company that is pioneering a new Behavior Consequence Management technology. He also is a cofounder of MyPoints.com (Nasdaq: MYPT), a wildly popular online consumer incentive program used by more than 3.5 million people. Muller was practically born to do performance and loyalty programs. His family jump-started the incentive industry in the 1950s, founding the famed Gold Stamps program and National Incentive Advertising. Muller has devoted the past five years to integrating his family's traditional marketing expertise with emerging strategies for the Internet. In January 1999 Muller left MyPoints.com to try his hand at the business-to-business behavior-based performance industry. CultureWorx, founded in January 1999, is an Internet-based performance management system for companies with employee-dense business units. The Mount Prospect company has leveraged the latest Internet technology to create a program that offers prompt, personalized reinforcement via the Internet for behaviors and activities that align with corporate strategy – a new management paradigm known as Behavior Consequence Management. Prior to developing online products, Muller honed his marketing acumen as a senior consultant. He conducted high-level project management for prestigious clients such as Sears and General Motors. Muller also is the co-founder of Warm Blankets, a not-for-profit organization developing and working with orphanages around the world. He has a B.A. in Marketing from DePaul University.

Andrew Goldsmith

Andrew Goldsmith, formerly a reporter at The Providence (R.I.) Journal, has published articles in Fortune and Fast Company. He is the author of *OneHourWiz: Landing Your First Job*, also published by Aspatore Books. He is now a J.D. student at Harvard Law School.

For information on speaking opportunities, interviews, or more information on the authors or the topics mentioned in this book, please email authors@aspatore.com.

**ASPATORE
BOOKS**